Tales from
Gombe

Tales from
Gombe

Anup Shah and Fiona Rogers

FIREFLY BOOKS

FOR THE BROTHERS: FRODO AND FREUD

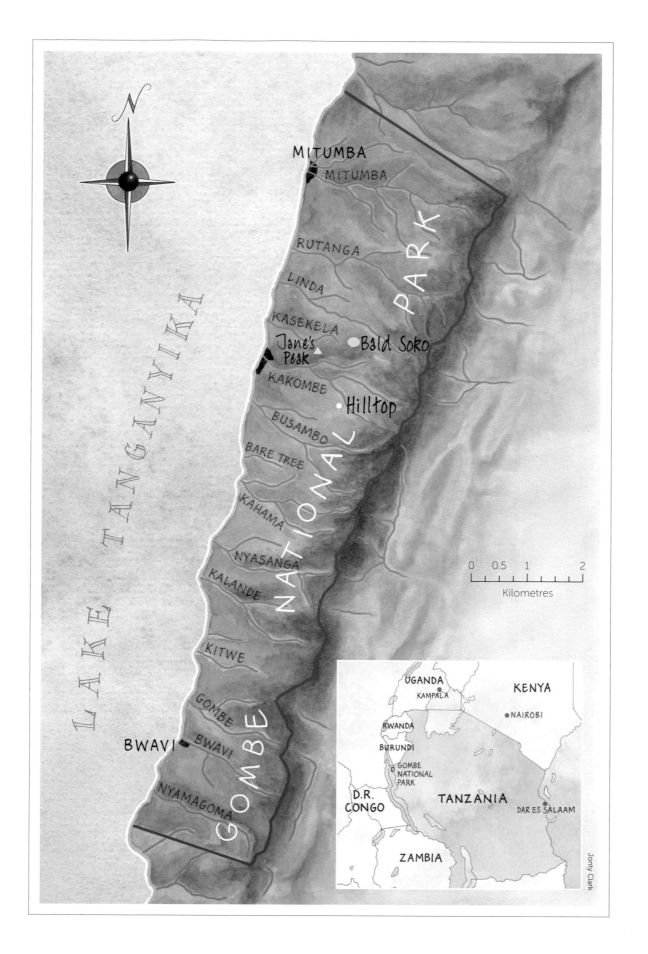

Gombe National Park is in western Tanzania on the shore of Lake Tanganyika. It is home to probably the most famous group of wild animals in history, the Gombe chimpanzees, whose lives have been observed and chronicled for over 50 years. Through studies initiated by paleontologist and anthropologist Louis Leakey and carried out by primatologist Dr Jane Goodall, people worldwide know their names and stories.

A FIREFLY BOOK

Published by Firefly Books Ltd. 2014

First printing

Publisher Cataloging-in-Publication Data (U.S.)

Shah, Anup.
   Tales from Gombe / Anup Shah ; and Fiona Rogers.
[320] pages : col. photos. ; cm.
Includes index.
Summary: "Anup Shah and Fiona Rogers have spent much of the last decade in the company of the world-famous chimpanzees of Tanzania's Gombe National Park, getting to know their characters and learning about the intricacies of their lives. Tales from Gombe provides an unparalled insight into their world. Through endearing stories and stunningly intimate photography, it tells the story of their lives, an epic saga full of convoluted plots, family alliances, intrigue, love, passion, suffering, ambition, politics, puzzles, surprises and controversies." -- Provided by publisher.
ISBN-13: 978-1-77085-468-0
1. Chimpanzees – Behavior – Tanzania – Gombe National Park. 2. Gombe National Park (Tanzania). I. Rogers, Fiona. II. Title.
599.88440451 dc23 QL737.P96.S434 2014

Library and Archives Canada Cataloguing in Publication

Shah, Anup, 1949–, author, photographer
   Tales from Gombe / Anup Shah and Fiona Rogers.
"First published by the Natural History Museum Cromwell Road, London SW7 5BD"—title page verso.
Includes bibliographical references.
ISBN 978-1-77085-468-0 (bound)
   1. Chimpanzees—Behavior—Tanzania—Gombe National Park. 2. Chimpanzees—Behavior—Tanzania—Gombe National Park—Pictorial works. 3. Gombe National Park (Tanzania). 4. Gombe National Park (Tanzania) —Pictorial works. 5. Photography of animals. I. Rogers, Fiona (Photographer), author, photographer II. Title. III. Title: Gombe.
QL737.P96S53 2014   599.88509669'84   C2014-901116-4

Published in the United States by
Firefly Books (U.S.) Inc.
P.O. Box 1338, Ellicott Station
Buffalo, New York 14205

Published in Canada by
Firefly Books Ltd.
50 Staples Avenue, Unit 1
Richmond Hill, Ontario L4B 0A7

Reproduction by Saxon Digital Services
Printed by C&C Offset, China

Acknowledgments
We would like to thank Iddi Kaluse, our skillful guide, Fidel Dotto Nyabenda our remarkable tracker, Anthony Collins for all his ingenious help, Roz Kidman Cox for her enthusiastic support, Colin Ziegler for sharing and refining our vision, and Simon Bishop for his sympathetic design.

Note
The ages mentioned in the captions are those at the time a given photograph was taken.

First published by
the Natural History Museum
Cromwell Road, London SW7 5BD

Designed by Simon Bishop

Contents

The brothers: 42-year-old Freud (right) and
37-year-old Frodo (above). They played together
as kids, teamed up as juveniles, fought each other
when young adults and eased into their societal
niches as elders.

Pax in the forest. Pax, sitting apart, is waiting to follow the big males when they've finished resting and have decided to move on. Pax is a small male who doesn't have the respect of the big males. He is tolerated by them, but they do not regard him as one of them. On the other hand, Pax probably knows the forest better than any of them.

The impromptu dance. It was peaceful that mid-morning, and everyone was very laid back. Faustino, a very high-ranking male, chose that time to make an impact on the others by displaying, prompting everyone in the vicinity to get out of the way as quickly as possible. Within 15 seconds the display was over and peace reigned once again, but a point had been reiterated about Faustino's high standing in the society.

Similar yet different. Brothers 42-year-old Freud (above) and
24-year-old Faustino (right) share a genetic heritage but have very
different temperaments. Freud often looked after Faustino when he
was a youngster, but volatile, high-ranking Faustino once pounded
on gentle, lower-ranking Freud when he dared ask for meat from
another younger brother, Ferdinand. Thus Freud was told that he
was only entitled to meat that Ferdinand chose to dispense.

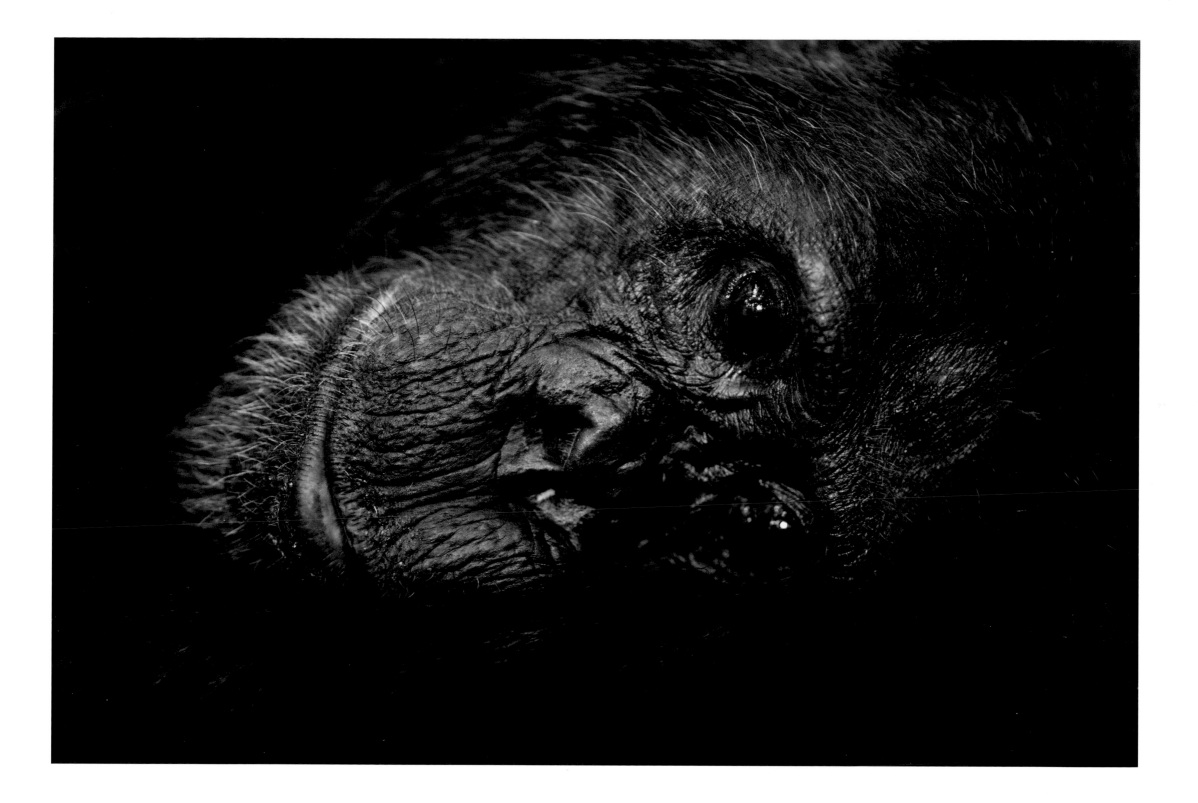

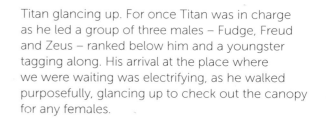

Titan glancing up. For once Titan was in charge
as he led a group of three males – Fudge, Freud
and Zeus – ranked below him and a youngster
tagging along. His arrival at the place where
we were waiting was electrifying, as he walked
purposefully, glancing up to check out the canopy
for any females.

Gimli lying with fruit on chest. With seasonal fruit at hand, members of the G family gorged themselves and then the adults went termite-fishing. Gimli couldn't be bothered to engage in an activity that takes so much patience and concentration. Instead, he carried a bunch of fruit to a comfortable spot covered with dry leaves and near the busy adults. He put the fruit on his chest and ate slowly, enjoying the Roman-style decadence.

Lost to the world, Golden and Glamour fast asleep. It was a long walk, but finally the small party of Kasekelians arrived at the targeted fruit source and fed ravenously. Feast over, Golden suckled her baby Glamour and then mother and daughter cuddled up for a nap.

Eight-year-old Gimli calling. The Kasekelians were at a high elevation where they decided to rest a while. Gremlin and her sons spent the time grooming each other. Then, when the males called, Gremlin's son, Gimli, reacted instinctively and eagerly, calling as hard as he could. Gimli is fascinated by the big males and can't wait to be one himself.

Preface

There lives a society far away that we came to know. It imposes fewer inhibitions on its citizens than perhaps any other society. There are very few cultural constraints on the appearance and behaviour of its members. The meagre rules of conduct that do exist are implicit and well understood. These norms are almost always followed, so there are no policemen, judges or lawyers. This society is a fine example of self-regulated social conduct.

As a consequence, its members have had no need to create a mask to impress the world. Their eccentricities and their idiosyncrasies have had the chance to develop in the confines of their society, and it does not occur to them that they have anything to conceal. So they express their oddities, personalities and emotions without inhibition, and you can't but help admire their frankness and openness.

We observed the members of this society over long periods of time. We came to realise that since they expressed themselves freely, there was a wide diversity of personalities. We found it difficult to use scientific methods to analyse, categorise and measure them. Indeed, it would have been a distortion of the truth to reduce our observations to data. So all the analytical tools we had been brought up with were rendered useless and, in fact, would have been misleading had we applied them.

We also struggled to find another society to which we could reference them. We came to realise that just as the individuals in this society are unique personalities, the society itself is unique. We had to have a seismic shift in our mind-sets. Thus we now think that a study of a tribe cannot be done properly. Perhaps there is no such thing as 'the tribe nature' or 'the tribe condition' or, by extension, 'human nature' and 'the human condition'. These are concepts we cling to because, perhaps, we prefer easy thinking to complex reality; we prefer reducing diversity to suit the limitations of our thinking abilities. We now believe that there are only stories of individuals, their unique struggles and triumphs and their unique interactions. Fortunately, we are photographers and have learnt to observe with a different eye. As photographers, we are not constrained by the strict requirements of modern science to study the minutiae. We can view a society as a whole.

Thus liberated, we shed our assumptions, discarded our analytical tools, opened our eyes wide and saw riches all around.

Frodo walking on a track. It's the dry season, which lasts from May to mid-October, and Frodo is walking steadily on a leaf-covered trail with a bunch of fruit stuffed in his mouth. A mesmerised youngster, Gimli, is trailing him at a respectful distance.

The big and the beautiful: Titan (above) and Faustino (right).
Titan is the heaviest Kasekelian. He commands respect from
the females but not affection; you can sense that they are a
little apprehensive of him – with reason, since Titan has an
unpredictable temper. On the other hand, Faustino, who is big
but not as big as Titan, is a favourite of the females. Faustino Is
Titan's uncle and outranks him in the male hierarchy.

Apollo on the move. We were waiting near a
mgwiza tree and a few female Kasekelians were
feeding on its fruit. Apollo, a 32-year-old male,
chanced by. He was on his own. He sat near us and
scanned the tree. On not finding any males there,
he moved on. He wasn't hungry for fruit; he was
seeking male company.

Titan leading Sandi and her family. A small group
of Kasekelians is on the move. Titan is catching
up with the leaders and is followed by Sandi,
the fourth oldest Kasekelian, her son Siri and
another youngster. In a mixed group like this, the
Kasekelians travel during daylight hours to get from
one food source to another. Border patrols are
normally, although not always, carried out by an
all-male group.

The rivals: Ferdinand (above) and Titan (right). Their
mothers were friends, they themselves are of a
similar age, and they grew up together as friends.
But as adults not much love is lost between them.
They are rivals for status and while Titan is more
powerful physically, Ferdinand is the shrewder of
the two.

Chapter 1: **The F, G and T Dynasties**

You can think of Kasekela as a village without a permanent structure. Several dynasties going back many many years live here within a forest called Gombe. I first came here at the beginning of the twenty-first century to catch a glimpse of those lives lived. I didn't know then that I would be so captivated by the personalities I met that I would return time and time again and, more recently, with my wife Fiona.

Gombe Forest rises steeply from the shores of Lake Tanganyika in Tanzania. To reach it you undertake a journey of 12 miles by boat from the sleepy town of Kigoma. The lake is normally calm in the morning, but in the strong wind of the afternoon, it ripples with waves. In the rainy season, when a heavy downpour clears the air of haze, you can see the outlines of the hills of the Congo to the west. Far, far north, along the shore of this seemingly endless lake, is the state of Burundi. The eastern shore, which the boat stays close to as it chugs along, is forested, except where the surface is rocky and the topsoil too thin.

Although there is a pronounced dry season from mid-May to early October, the forest is always lush. Its inhabitants, at first, are difficult to see, and it's also hard to tell one individual from another. But if you stay with them for a long time, as we have been doing, then you get to know them and realise how different they are from each other. As an unexpected bonus, you also glimpse the intricate webs of their relationships.

The Community is dominated by a few dynasties, and on my first full day in the forest back in 2001, I encountered Fifi of the F dynasty. She was with two of her sons and one of her daughters. She was nearly 43 years old then but went about her daily tasks with the ease and agility of one 20 years younger, or so it seemed.

Gombe Forest is dissected by a number of streams running parallel to each other from the hills in the east to the lake in the west. For ease of identifying a location,

each section of the forest is named after the river flowing through it. I learnt that Fifi normally ranged in Kasekela valley and the adjoining Kakombe valley and that the Community she belonged to was known as the Kasekela Community.

Fifi, I also learnt, had considerable clout in the Community. In fact, she was at the top of the female social hierarchy. But she had started life with a social advantage. Her mother, Flo, was high-ranking, as were her two elder brothers. In fact, one of them, Figan, had held the leadership of the Community on and off for nearly nine years, a record. So Fifi grew up surrounded by confident and assertive elders, and this must have given her a leg up in the female hierarchy. And, looking into her eyes, I could also detect a keen intelligence.

Fifi was a successful mother, too. She bore nine offspring, of which seven made it to adulthood. Fifi's mother, Flo, was a good mother herself, and Fifi learnt her mothering skills by observing Flo. She seemed to possess a natural aptitude for mothering. From an early age, she could never resist expertly holding, grooming and carrying her baby brother.

The first day I saw Fifi – such a long time ago it seems now, in February 2001 – she was in a tree, feeding on fruit that had come into season. One of her sons, 12-year-old Faustino, was down on the ground and he momentarily glanced at me. How different he looked from the Faustino that is the puzzle today. Then, secure in the presence of Fifi nearby, he was quietly confident and controlled. Social status wasn't at the front of his mind then.

As Fifi continued feeding, engrossed in making the most of the bounty in the tree, a shape detached from her and climbed into an adjoining tree using the branches interlocking the two trees. This was Flirt, Fifi's daughter, then two and half years old. Like all the F dynasty members, she was big. I recall that she was playful, bold and confident. But when we sat with Flirt recently, more than a decade later, we noticed a subtle change. She was quiet and subdued.

Over the course of ten years I came to learn that Flirt and Faustino had less influence on the shape of the Kasekela Community's recent history than four other members of the F dynasty. I remember coming across two of them a few days after my first encounter with Fifi. One of them was 30-year-old Freud, walking leisurely along a forest trail, followed by his younger brother, eight-and-a-half-year-old Ferdinand. Freud was Fifi's first-born, and Ferdinand her youngest son.

Freud exuded calm, quiet confidence. I later learnt that he was something of a loner who, when he did get involved socially, always did so on his terms. He came and went as he chose, sometimes with either Faustino or Ferdinand or both trailing him. An enigmatic character, Freud has a rich history.

During that first encounter with Freud and Ferdinand, Freud decided to rest for a while. He sat down and struck up his characteristic pose of Freud the thinker. Ferdinand also stopped and struck his own thinking pose. I settled down and together we sat for about 15 minutes. The lake was calm and the only noise I could hear was the soft chirruping of a few invisible insects. It felt as if I was living in humanity's distant past.

Thinking about Ferdinand and knowing what I know now, it seems even way back then he had a plan, and following, watching and thinking like Freud seems to have been part of that plan. Looking at Ferdinand today, a far cry from the lithe, slender boy tagging after his elder brother, I am astonished at how far he has come. Then, it was elder brother Faustino who was expected to achieve what Ferdinand finally accomplished.

Our evening descent to the rest house was uneventful except for a troop of red colobus monkeys that travelled overhead through the forest canopy. Back at the rest house, watching the fiery sun set over the calm lake, I went over Freud's past. Baby Freud, born in 1971, not only had an eager first-time mother in Fifi but also the care and support of his grandmother, Flo, and his two high-ranking uncles. With these two around to pat his head and ruffle his hair, it's not surprising that Freud developed a fascination with the big males of the Community. As an infant he would watch them, filled with wonder, and when he was able to walk he would totter up to greet any male that happened by. Often, unsteady on his feet yet still unable to resist the temptation, he would try to follow a departing male, much to Fifi's bemusement.

When Freud was seven, the urge to dominate other Kasekelians began to surface and he worked out a plan to that end. He began by challenging the older juveniles whose mothers were of lower rank than Fifi. These were shrewd targets because if one of the mothers turned on him to protect her offspring, Fifi would come charging in to back him up. Once Freud had subjugated all the youngsters, he turned his attention to mature females. Although this created a headache for Fifi, in this project, too, she invariably backed him up. And through all this, Freud was growing bigger and stronger. By the time he was nine, he was able to back Fifi in turn whenever she had a disagreement with another female.

Thus, together, mother and son consolidated their high social standing among the females. During their travels in the forest, given Fifi's sociable nature, Freud and Fifi joined many gatherings. Such gatherings provided Freud with opportunities to gain social capital. In particular, he learned to read the body language of the males and male group dynamics: the moods, the simmering tensions and the sudden aggressions that erupted so unexpectedly and dramatically.

Thus Freud learnt, and with education came confidence. Slowly but inevitably, he went to the edge of his mother's security zone and eventually, though still very young, he crossed the boundary and entered the world of the adult males.

As Freud continued to grow physically and mentally, he also aggressively climbed the male hierarchy. But his personality appeared gradually to change. By the time he was 17, he had become very laid back, as if shorn of all ambition. Often he would be found sitting alone, hand supporting chin, gazing into nothing. If undisturbed, he would hold that pose for about 15 minutes. Perhaps he was meditating. He seemed to be content with being a top-ranking male, second only to the then leader, Wilkie.

It was also in 2001, on a cloudy February morning threatening rain, that I first encountered 28-year-old Wilkie. That day we had not found any Kasekelians to start with, so we waited and listened. Looking up through the rustling leaves, I saw some lithe, sleek red-tailed monkeys moving silently. A lone male baboon barked. After about half an hour, we heard loud calls. Judging by the volume, some Kasekelians were about half a mile away. We headed toward the source of the sound and found Wilkie sitting with the other males, seemingly lost in thought. I remember his wise face and shrewd eyes. As time has passed, little seemed to change in that visage. If anything, there was even more history written on it.

Wilkie was the son of Winkle and Evered. They were his only adult relatives, and then Evered passed away. Despite having the active support of only his mother, Wilkie rose through the ranks. By way of cunning, tactical alliances and sheer opportunism, he became the leader at age 17 and ruled for three to four years. Incidentally, it was when he was six months away from the leadership that he mated with Fifi and Faustino was subsequently born.

No matter. Though Freud gave the impression that he wasn't interested in being the leader, he was actually just waiting for a chance to dethrone Wilkie. For when Freud was 21, he caught Wilkie by surprise and was able to defeat him convincingly, thus becoming the Kasekelian leader himself.

After his dethronement, Wilkie was actually kicked out of the Community by the males he had lorded it over and was forced into exile. He wasn't cut out for a lonely existence, though. Being social and male, Wilkie longed to be part of the social scene where females are also present. But he was also afraid of being caught by a group of males who might be inclined to punish him, perhaps out of spite.

Finally, after two or three years in exile, the loneliness got too much for Wilkie, and one day he cautiously walked over to a group of males that included Freud. Without hesitation, they advanced upon him with Freud in the lead. Displaying all the signs of submission that he could muster – crouching, squeaking appeasing noises, grinning – Wilkie nervously braced himself for the worst. Then, unexpectedly, Freud started grooming Wilkie, signalling reconciliation. A group grooming session ensued, with Wilkie a part of it. Thus Wilkie's re-establishment into the Community began. Over time, and frequent grooming sessions with high ranking males, Wilkie quietly secured his place in the Community, although he never again achieved high rank, something that didn't appear to bother him.

It's at transforming moments such as this – Freud signalling peace with Wilkie – that you can glimpse the depth of Freud's wisdom. The social norm is not very clear here; the outcast is either badly beaten or forgiven. Freud chose reconciliation.

All that happened in 1993 and much has changed since. One agent of change was Frodo, Fifi's second eldest son and Freud's younger brother.

In that first visit to Kasekela Community that I made in 2001, several days had passed without my meeting up with 25-year-old Frodo. Then, one hazy morning, I found him on the lower slopes of the forest, gorging on leaves. Even without sighting him, I could smell him, a distinctive waft of unmistakable odour, quite pleasant actually. The first view I had of him was his huge back. But then, from whatever angle I looked at him he appeared massive. He had bulging shoulders and arms and a mean glint in his eyes. Frodo had been a big baby and had simply grown and grown until he was the second heaviest Kasekelian ever recorded.

Right from an early age Frodo was fascinated by everything that elder brother Freud did. He also imitated Freud's macho behaviour. For example, when Frodo was only nine months old and still unsteady on his feet, he watched Freud perform an impressive display and then attempted an imitation himself, falling over in the process. Then, whenever Freud displayed in front of the females, little Frodo joined in, lips pursed, hair bristling, stamping on unsteady legs, swinging tiny branches, looking purposeful but harmless. You could say that Frodo hero-worshipped Freud.

Freud, in turn, was Frodo's self-appointed guardian. Thus, if Frodo happened to climb an imposing tree and got stuck, Freud would rescue his whimpering kid brother. When, at the age of 10, Freud started travelling through the forest with the big males, five-year-old Frodo would sometimes accompany him for a day or two, trusting his older brother to hold his hand.

As Frodo grew, he rapidly ascended the male hierarchy and, by the time he was 17, only the leader, elder brother Freud, outranked him. It then seemed that Frodo, at the mercy of his imperatives, had no choice but to go for the leadership himself and so the stage was set for an unusual tussle between brother and brother, mentor and pupil.

Before describing that, I would like to mention the one personality in the F dynasty who has always been likely to have a disproportionate influence on the future course of the Community – Fanni, the third eldest of Fifi's children. One day, during that first visit to the Kasekela Community, after propelling ourselves through tangles, vines, thorns and saplings, we came across Fanni picking her way through the forest, carrying one child while another followed obediently. I was at once struck by how much she looked like Fifi. In her personality, though, she has always been very different from her mother.

12 years ago Fanni had two kids in tow; two years ago she had three. Having a total of five children is quite impressive, and you could easily believe that Fanni has been an excellent mother. That's more or less true now, but it wasn't always. Consider this: Fanni gave birth to Fax, a male infant, when she was only 11 years old. She didn't have a clue how to pick up her baby, how to cradle him or how to carry him. She also repeatedly failed to respond to his cries for attention. You could accurately say that she was negligent, but you could as easily say that she was young and carefree. In any case, Fax died, cause unknown. However, when Fudge was born in December 1996, Fanni was older and had become interested in mothering. She stayed close to Fifi and picked up some useful maternal skills. Consequently, today Fudge seems to be doing well, even though his mental development, at one point, had a twist.

What happened was this: Fanni gave birth to Fundi when Fudge was only three and a half and still highly dependent on her. Sadly for Fudge, Fanni became so engrossed in Fundi that she neglected him. Once, for example, she climbed a tree with baby Fundi that was too difficult for little Fudge to scale. So he cried and screamed, sitting at the base of the tree. Yet Fanni didn't come down to fetch him. Instead, she ignored him completely.

Fudge had problems adjusting to the new situation. A sensitive soul, he became listless and depressed. No longer the centre of Fanni's world, he withdrew into himself and swapped playing for brooding. Life seemed to have gone out of his body.

Meanwhile, life for Fundi was joyous. At six months, he was the youngest member of the F dynasty and received much attention and affection from his relatives. Then, when he was a little older, Fanni allowed him to play with other youngsters of the Community and, as a result, matters improved for Fudge. Fanni had more time to spare, some of which she used to groom Fudge to his obvious delight. Furthermore, if they were travelling and Fudge lingered en route, she started to wait for him to catch up. Fudge perked up and the threesome appeared more cohesive and much more at ease with one another.

Watching the F dynasty then, such a long time ago, I realised that since there were nine of them altogether – Fifi, her four sons and two daughters (I have not mentioned Flossi, who emigrated at maturity) and two grandsons – they constituted one sixth of the Community. The F clan was clearly a powerful force, with Freud as the Community's leader and Fifi the top-ranking female. Moreover, the clan's number was set to rise, thanks to Fanni's fertility.

Fanni was and is an enigma. Despite being Fifi's daughter, she wasn't high-ranking. Perhaps this was due to the rough handling she received from elder brother Frodo when an infant: she could never be sure whether Frodo was playing with her or bullying her. Fifi never intervened when play got out of hand, and Fanni had to cope as best as she could. Even when grown up, Fanni was not sure about Frodo. Quite recently, Fiona and I were watching Fanni with her kids when Frodo came along at speed, slapped a cowering Fanni and continued on his way. Without doubt, Frodo did not bring out Fanni's sociable side.

Fanni is also a bit of a loner. She ventures off on her own through the forest for days on end, with just her kids for company. Now, as then, she is often found settled somewhere with her kids close to her, a vacant expression on her face as if she's day-dreaming. Maybe Fanni doesn't care about rank. With her largely lonesome lifestyle, what good is high rank? And there's a dark side to Fanni.

This dark side was revealed very dramatically when an unusual event (related in Chapter 6) occurred involving a Kasekelian female called Gremlin. She was the daughter of Melissa and Evered, the same Evered who sired Wilkie. One balmy day, during my first visit to the Kasekela Community, after we had walked up and down two valleys, tripping over roots and being hit by low branches, we found Gremlin. She was sitting there, looking around. She scratched her belly slowly and deliberately and then assumed a purposeful demeanour, walking over to a clump of grass. Here she carefully selected and trimmed a grass blade. Then, holding it in her mouth, she set off for a termite mound that was completely out of sight. Upon arrival, she inspected the mound and began a fishing session. She scratched at the plugged tunnels of the mound until she found portals into the mound's interior and then gently inserted the modified grass blade into a tunnel. Quite quickly, almond-coloured soldier termites latched onto the tool with their powerful mandibles. She gingerly withdrew the probe from the mound so that the dozens of termites clinging precariously to it weren't knocked off. Then, she drew the blade between her lips and crunched the termites. Gremlin thus caught and ate about seven termites a minute, or a stomach-tickling 400 in that hour-long fishing session.

Of the three major maternal dynasties in today's Kasekela Community, Gremlin's – the G dynasty – is the second biggest. This is surprising because Gremlin did not get off to a good start as a mother, losing her first three children. She gave birth to Getty in 1982 and after four years something terrible happened: in early July 1986 Getty's body was found minus his head. Gremlin gave birth again in 1987, but then Gremlin herself became seriously ill and her unnamed infant died. Gremlin recovered and gave birth to Galahad in April 1988, but in 2000 he, too, passed away at the age of 12 of a suspected respiratory infection.

In June 1992, 22-year-old Gremlin and 20-year-old Wilkie, then in the last phase of his reign, got together and mated. This was rather shocking since Gremlin and Wilkie had the same father, Evered. The mating was successful and Gremlin's fourth child, Gaia, was born in February 1993.

When I first saw eight-year-old Gaia she came across as just a little girl. From what I recall during the several days I spent with Gremlin and Gaia, she was neat, unfussy and a great help to Gremlin. She also made it a rule to stay out of social dramas and therefore out of trouble. This rule she still follows today, particularly after some bizarre events in her life.

Back then, Gaia was busy looking after her younger twin sisters, Glitter and Golden. But it wasn't always so. Gaia was five and a half years old and still a mummy's girl when Gremlin gave birth to the twins, sired by Frodo. With their arrival, Gaia's world changed. Previously she was Gremlin's pride and joy, but now she felt neglected. Before the twins' arrival Gremlin readily obliged when Gaia requested grooming. But now, with the tiny twins literally filling her hands, Gremlin ignored Gaia's plea for a scratch. However, that posed a dilemma for Gremlin because Gaia was prone then to throw a tantrum, which upset the twins. Then, when Gaia was just seven years old, her whole attitude changed.

This change was triggered by a mysterious virus that hit the Kasekelians in the summer of 1999. It's difficult to tell how such an infection travels and finds weaknesses, but they all had symptoms of the respiratory infection. Frodo, physically the strongest Kasekelian, fell seriously ill, in fact too ill to move. For three days he slept alone in a well hidden place. Even when a few baboons chanced upon him and came close enough to touch him, he didn't flex a muscle. In the end, he made a full recovery, but some Kasekelians didn't. No one can tell why, but Gaia's personality was transformed after the virus had done its worst and gone. She appointed herself nanny to the twins, and Gremlin allowed her to handle them as she pleased. Gaia, at seven, was still a child herself and she delighted in playing with the twins. They, in turn, relished the attention they got from their elder sister.

Gaia was an expert at termite-fishing. Glitter was fascinated by this activity and picked it up quickly both by watching Gremlin and Gaia fish and practising assiduously herself. Golden, the other twin, initially preferred stealing termites from her mother and sister, but she eventually became adept at it too.

The twins started life with a size disadvantage. Flirt, who was born nearly a month after the twins, was huge in comparison. However, despite their small size, Gremlin found it hard to bring them up. Moving and climbing up trees with twins was tough going and, even when she was at rest, the twins needed suckling, grooming and cuddling. Fortunately, with Gaia chipping in, Gremlin coped to such an extent that the twins had reached normal size by the time they were three years old.

With Gaia attending to the twins, Gremlin was able to relax a little, although she always kept an eye on the threesome. This was especially necessary when seven-year-old Titan was around. Play could turn rough surprisingly quickly, and then Gaia would shriek for the sake of the twins and Gremlin would be there in no time, chasing the insolent youngster away.

Titan was an irrepressible youngster with energy to spare. But what struck me most when I first saw him was his size – for his age, he was bigger than normal. Probably his size was inherited from his parents. Tatti was huge and his father Frodo was a giant. Moreover, from quite early on Titan displayed Frodo-like behaviour, such as indiscriminately throwing stones and rocks and playing dare with baboons. He also spent some of his vast reservoir of energy playing crazy, inventive games. His frantic and boisterous play quickly wore down his playmates and made life hell for those who yearned for a bit of peace and quiet – especially his mother Tatti and his normally easy-going elder sister, 12-year-old Tanga.

Tanga has a relaxed demeanour. From adolescence onwards, she often used to hang around with Fifi, though very much in her shadow. I can remember an incident that clearly demonstrated Tanga's deference to Fifi. The two were travelling with their kids when they chanced upon a termite mound. Eagerly, Fifi looked around and found a grass stem which she modified and used to fish. Tanga sat and watched from a distance. Only after half an hour had elapsed and Fifi had moved on did Tanga began termite-fishing herself.

Tanga had her first baby in 2001 – a boy called Tom, whose father was a high-ranking male called Kris. Although Tom was her first baby, Tanga was quite laid back about Tom's safety. From a very early age he would be allowed to go off to play by himself and mix freely with the others. As an infant and then as a juvenile, Tom was healthy, social, playful and bold.

Tanga's father was Goblin, elder brother of Gremlin and a figure with a rich history. Goblin had become the leader of the Community through sheer persistence. Tenaciously, he had then stayed at the top for a long spell. After being overthrown by Wilkie, he had revealed his diplomatic side by forming shrewd alliances with high-ranking males. Thus he made friends with Wilkie after his downfall and enjoyed all the associated privileges. Then he did the same with Freud when he became the leader. However, when 17-year old Frodo began to vie for the leadership, Goblin didn't commit himself to either the current leader, Freud, or the rising star, Frodo. As for the lesser Kasekelians, Goblin made sure he was respected by putting on intimidating displays.

Way back then I had made four long visits to The Kasekela Community between February 2001 and October 2003. A lot happened in my life after those visits, including meeting my wife, Fiona, a wildlife photographer with class. She was as intrigued as I was about the Kasekela personalities and happenings. We finally succumbed to the spell of that far-off land and paid a month-long visit in June 2011 to renew acquaintances and to find out what had happened to Freud, Frodo, Goblin, Gremlin, her twins and all the others in the intervening years.

Tarzan at peak. Gombe Forest rises steeply to about 300 metres above the shores of Lake Tanganyika. Beyond that height the tree roots can't get a grip in the thin topsoil and the forested slopes give way to grass and bare patches interspersed with rocks.

Fifi with her two-day-old baby, Furaha. When
44-year-old Fifi gave birth to her ninth baby,
Furaha, it came as a surprise: she was very old for
a Kasekelian. Equally surprising was the radiant
health of mother and baby. Fifi's four-year-old
daughter Flirt was with Fifi when Furaha was born,
but her other offspring only found out a few days
later. They were utterly fascinated by Furaha and
protective of mother and baby – not that Fifi
needed any protection.

Then: 12-year-old Faustino feeding. There was a certain air of quiet bravado about Faustino then, especially when he was with his mother Fifi, the top-ranking female. His confidence grew when his two elder brothers were also around, and he was already dominant over all the adolescents and quite a few adult females. On his way up the rankings, Faustino was being thought of as a potential leader.

Now: 24-year-old Faustino, the enigma. Faustino today is very confident but doesn't seem ambitious. Already a high-ranking male, he appears to be quite content with his lot. At times, he appears gentle and affectionate, but there are also times when he appears out of control, terrifying every Kasekelian in the vicinity. You might say that Faustino is quite moody.

Then: Freud, at 31, with his characteristic pose – the thinker. Watching him, you could see him think. Even as a youngster Freud demonstrated a knack for thinking out solutions to problems. He was the one who would steal baby sister Flossi when he wanted to move on but Fifi wanted to stay. Fifi would have to get up to catch a fleeing Freud with Flossi clung to his belly, and once up she would walk behind Freud who would then relinquish Flossi.

Now: Freud, at 42, still thinking. Freud seems to have lost some of his muscle power but none of his mental power. As always, Freud observes, then plans and finally acts. Astute as ever, he also deals with the members of the Community on his terms. Popular and respected, he comes and goes as he chooses.

Then: ten-year-old Ferdinand struck up his own pensive
pose while waiting for elder brother, Freud, to make a move.
Ferdinand was a skinny lad who gave the impression of being
quite unremarkable. Yet, if you observed him closely, you could
discern some remarkable traits. For one, he was a good observer
who followed, watched and learnt from his elder brothers,
especially from the social situations they got into and controlled.

Now: 20-year-old Ferdinand has filled out and is no longer the slim, lanky lad of ten years earlier. And he is not only more muscular, he is astute at social affairs thanks to his ability to read situations instantly. Every social act he performs seems to have a purpose, calculated to obtain a result. He also has one attribute that all those who aspire to political dominance should have – a ruthless streak.

Then: 29-year-old Wilkie. Wilkie then was reserved, content to look back on a life full of ups and downs. Coming from an unprivileged family, he had compensated by strength of character. There was nothing particularly impressive about him physically; he was just a medium-sized adult with brains. But he was ambitious and cunning and could command support and respect. He climbed up the male hierarchy rapidly and, after winning an epic fight with Goblin, the then leader, he ruled for nearly four years.

Now: 39-year-old Wilkie. Little seems to have changed in Wilkie's visage. If anything, his face has even more history written on it. Spending time with him, I found him to be as shrewd as ever and a popular figure with the females. Not surprisingly, Wilkie has sired the highest number of offspring in Kasekela of any male since records began.

Then: Frodo. I had heard about Frodo and his ruthless demonstrations of power when I first set foot in Kasekela. The reality didn't disappoint. I encountered Frodo, then 25, one hazy morning on the lower slopes of the forest, munching on leaves. From whatever angle I looked at him, he appeared massive. What I found particularly evident was his boundless confidence. Frodo wielded absolute power which he executed ruthlessly. He didn't have allies, apart from the Machiavellian Goblin; but then, he didn't need them.

Now: Frodo. When I saw 36-year-old Frodo, ten years after I had first met him, I recognized him at once but was taken aback by the physical changes. His face, which now had character written on it, was longer, his body was slimmer and his hair greyer. He gave the impression of being a wise, senior citizen. Two aspects of Frodo were still the same: he didn't groom anyone and his appetite for food was undiminished.

Then: Fudge. When I first came across four-year-old
Fudge, always in the shadow of his mother Fanni
and younger brother Fundi, he appeared to be very
downbeat. Serious in demeanour, he hardly played.
But he was a deep thinker.

Now: Fudge. Today 16-year-old Fudge brims with
confidence. He gets along with everyone: the kids
adore him, the females love him, and the males take
him seriously.

Then: Fundi. As Fanni called, 16-month-old Fundi sat oblivious in his mother's lap. The group that Fanni was with had been resting and the time had come to move on. Presently, those in the lead called to the others to join them and Fanni replied. Back then, Fundi was the youngest member of the F dynasty and at the receiving end of much pampering. Fanni lavished affection on him and when Uncle Freud chanced to come along, he would condescend to ruffle Fundi's hair, while little Flirt would try to mother him. And there was always elder brother Fudge for Fundi to look up to.

Now: Fundi. Semi-independent Fundi, on his way to adulthood, is unsure of his place in the social order. He appears torn between the security of staying with Fanni and the option of mixing with the volatile and unpredictable adult males, as his instinct compels him to. He has found a middle way, though, by hanging around with his elder brother Fudge, who is asserting himself in the adult world.

Then: 22-year-old Fanni. She had a rough childhood, often being bullied by elder brother Frodo, who exceeded the limits of play with Fanni. As a young adult she was under the shadow of the dominant Fifi and, despite being top-ranking Fifi's eldest daughter, she herself was low-ranking. Fifi mixed freely socially but Fanni was somewhat misanthropic. With Fifi you could guess correctly at times what she was thinking, but with Fanni you could never tell. Sometimes I got the impression that Fanni had created a mental world into which she escaped whenever she chose.

Now: 32-year-old Fanni. She still doesn't appear to be interested in rank and is content to be away from social activities for long spells. Self-contained, she is happy to raise a family and she has been very successful, having given birth to six kids, four of which are still alive and asserting themselves in Kasekela society. You still can't read Fanni's face. Often she would glance at me, our eyes would meet, and I would see nothing.

Then: Fanni, Fundi and Fudge. Fanni had been walking with her two kids when she stopped to suckle Fundi, and Fudge quietly slipped into the background. Whenever I saw Fanni, she was always with two offspring and usually apart from the other Kasekelians.

Now: Fanni, Fifty and Fadhila. Fanni had again been walking with her two kids when she stopped to rest. Fifty and Fadhila, bored with waiting for Fanni to resume walking, started playing. I have yet to see Fanni on her own, and she continues to keep away from other Kasekelians for long spells.

Now: Gremlin. 41-year-old Gremlin's G dynasty is today the second largest in Kasekela. This is despite Gremlin losing her first three offspring. Her first-born, Getty, died aged four in mysterious circumstances involving foul play. Her second infant died without reaching its first birthday. Then she had Galahad,whose personality promised great things until he succumbed to a respiratory infection at age 12. The unusual thing about the G dynasty now is how well Gremlin holds it together.

Then: 31-year-old Gremlin. Gremlin has come through a lot of setbacks – the loss of her first three offspring and attacks from Fifi and Fanni. The latter attacks were paradoxical, since Gremlin and Fifi shared a home range and for the most part the two were very friendly. But then Fifi was older, was the top-ranking female and had sons who were successive leaders. So she could do pretty much what she liked, including pulling rank.

Then: Gaia. When I first saw Gaia she was eight years old and came across as a neat, tidy and calm character. She always seemed to be with Gremlin, her mother, helping her look after Gaia's three-year-old twin sisters. She would play with them, groom them and hasten them along whenever the males were around and showed signs of getting excited.

Now: Gaia. Nineteen-year-old Gaia has not changed much in personality. She continues to be unassuming, minding her own business. She now travels independently of Gremlin but they meet up frequently. Then they socialise, feed and travel together for a while. Sometimes, when they meet up after a long separation, their reunion tends to be quite emotional, with hugging thrown in. Gaia is still very loyal to Gremlin.

Then: the twins. Four-year-old twins, Golden (in front) and Glitter spur their mother Gremlin on as she accelerates through a forest clearing. Once, when the twins were only a few weeks old and fidgety, It had been tough for Gremlin to move. She had to hold both close to her chest with one arm and travel with her legs bent to support their backs with her thighs.

Now: the twins. In place of the two happy-go-lucky kids I remember, there are now two mature 14-year-olds. They are adults now but Golden (right) still has a mischievous look in her eyes and, every now and then, indulges in play for play's sake, while Glitter comes across as more serious – just one indication that their personalities are diverging.

Then: Glitter. The G family of four – Gremlin, Gaia and the twins – were on the move when one of the twins, Golden, dashed off into the thicker part of the forest, presumably to investigate something that must have caught her eye. Four-year-old Glitter, less impetuous than her twin, waited with her mother for Golden to return. Unlike Golden, Glitter was very observant.

Now: 13-year-old Glitter. She waits for twin Golden, who is busy grooming Frodo, their father. Glitter has grown up to be a cool, level-headed female with a toughness she rarely shows and an astute mind that she uses judiciously.

Then: Golden. The G Family was termite-fishing and, while the others got on with it, four-year-old Golden quickly gave up and waited. Early on in her life, Golden wasn't interested in termite fishing, preferring to steal termites from Gremlin. She did pick it up, though, and today she is skilled at it.

Now: Golden. Although the physical and behavioural changes in 14-year-old Golden are striking, she still has childlike traits such as playfulness. She is also closer to Gremlin than Glitter is and spends a considerable amount of time with her mother.

Then: Titan. What struck me when I first saw Titan was his size. Afterwards, I discovered that the eight-year-old was regularly exploding with energy. Even his sister – Tanga, five years older – would tire of playing with him. He would then think of games to play by himself with equal vigour. If an unlucky baboon ever chanced by, Titan would try to play with it, too. Usually the apprehensive baboon would run, whereupon Titan would pick up a stone, if one was around, and hurl it underarm at the retreating figure. His aim was utterly hopeless, though.

Now: 18 year-old Titan. He is the largest Kasekelian today, but his social skills need improvement. When he gets a surge of testosterone, he lays into the females. None of the males, with the possible exception of Faustino and younger brother Tarzan, are overtly friendly with him either. He also keeps away from elder sister Tanga. He still has considerable energy which he expends by relentless walking, alone.

Now: Tanga. Although less social than before, Tanga at 23 still appears chilled out and quite content with her lot in life. In a way she is much like Fanni, travelling with her kids in her own niche, not at all bothered by questions of position and status in society.

Then: 13-year-old Tanga: She had a relaxed air about her. It was as if she wasn't very bothered about anything. Tanga became independent of her mother, Tatti, fairly early on and then spent considerable time with Fifi. Nevertheless, whenever she encountered her mother, with Titan and Tarzan in tow, she would spend some time with them. You could say that she was sociable, had an independent streak and was carefree.

Then: One-year-old Tom. Tom was often left to
do as he pleased by his relaxed mother, Tanga,
including mixing with the Kasekelian kids who were
older than him. Being smaller than his playmates
didn't bother him in the least. In fact, he would
keep on playing even when it got rough. Tanga,
always nearby, couldn't be bothered.

Now: 12-year-old Tom. Today he has a mature-
looking face but a small body. A marked change
has come over him. He now appears to be a quiet,
serious sub-adult who is also quite emotional. He
is also very bold and quite capable of looking after
himself. Nevertheless, he lets his peers dominate
him.

Chapter 2: **Fifi's Boys: Freud vs Frodo**

It was early June 2011 when Fiona and I arrived at Kasekela. The rains had faltered by mid-May and subsequently petered out. Now the air was dry and the days were hot. Although the forest, which rose steeply from the lake shore, was thicker and lusher than I remembered it, the fruit crop was scarcer. We learned that the 60 Kasekelians, young and old, were scattered in pursuit of random sources of fruit.

We walked along streams, climbed steep slopes and descended into dark valleys, hoping to bump into Freud. Not surprisingly, he proved elusive. We learned that he still led an isolated life for long stretches of time, minding his own business, at ease with his own company, indulging in food, sleep and thought.

Then one evening, the calm of the forest was shattered by the arrival of a small band of males. Their presence created static in the air. Among them was Freud. That was so like him – to join up occasionally with the others, stay a short time and then quietly disappear without anyone noticing.

Freud's face looked battered – he wasn't handsome any more. A lot seemed to have happened since he was the leader and younger brother Frodo was number two.

At that time – the beginning of 1996 – Frodo was ambitious but was suffering from a handicap in that he had always looked up to Freud in awe. As time passed, over a year in fact, Frodo's ambition kept growing. He was clearly frustrated and let his frustrations spill over by bullying the others. However, he still hesitated to challenge his brother for the leadership and Freud knew this. So, to keep Frodo in check, Freud would occasionally pull rank.

There was the memorable instance when Frodo displayed in Freud's presence. Sensing that this could be insubordination, Freud himself worked up a display that left all the Kasekelians present awestruck. To drive the message home – I am in charge here – Freud waded into a stream and continued performing there. This really impressed the onlookers since all Kasekelians hate getting wet. Freud's bravado broke Frodo's nerve and he quickly retreated, whimpering, up a tree. To consolidate his psychological triumph, Freud chased a frightened Frodo from tree to tree until Frodo was, for all practical purposes, reduced to tears. At last, following his electrifying performance, Freud stopped and sat down, totally calm, beneath the tree Frodo had ended up in. After a while, Frodo descended gingerly, nervously edged towards Freud and started grooming him. Frodo had surrendered for now.

The problem for Freud was that the wiring in Frodo's brain wasn't hard enough. With each surge of testosterone, Frodo was tempted to flex his muscles once more. He stopped short of challenging Freud, but let off his bubbling exasperation by terrorising the other males and raping females. In fact, when Fifi gave birth to Freddi in September 1996, DNA analysis showed that the father was Frodo, her son.

Fifi didn't play king-maker. Whether Freud or Frodo, her son would be the leader. So, in typical Fifi fashion, she left them to their rivalry. She never interfered in their altercations. In fact, like every wise Kasekelian, she quickly got out of the way when they displayed, clutching infant Ferdinand while, under his own steam, young Faustino raced to safety. After all, when these two big boys displayed, Frodo, at least, could easily get out of control.

Then, one day, when Freud had been in charge for about three years, Frodo finally challenged him directly. Instead of displaying generally, he displayed at Freud himself. Initially, Freud ignored him, but Frodo escalated his display. So, as if with great reluctance, Freud got up. First, he psyched himself up by rocking from side to side, and then, with hair bristling, he launched into an unforgettable display aimed at Frodo. But for a change Frodo stood his ground and displayed in turn. Thus the brothers displayed at each other, using whatever props they could lay their hands on to accentuate their show of power. Frodo was physically stronger but, mentally, he was the weaker of the two. Freud unerringly found his mental weak spot with a virtuoso performance that broke Frodo's nerve. He scampered up a tree, signalling defeat. But Freud wasn't finished. He kept displaying under the tree, sending waves of fear through Frodo. When Freud was done, he left. After a while, Frodo climbed down and slunk away.

Goblin saw an opportunity in Freud's and Frodo's feud. He allied with either of them as circumstances dictated. Whenever Freud was away from the centre of community life, he sided with Frodo; but when Freud was around he sided with him. Goblin couldn't lose. He had access to any female that he had his eyes on and neither Freud nor Frodo would stop him lest they lose his support to the other.

Freud continued to rule with a light touch. Shrewd and diplomatic, he had no need to show aggression to keep order, unless someone was being insubordinate. There were young ambitious males around lusting for power, but Frodo was almost always the one to show any defiance. There was also another aspect to Freud's style of leadership; as mentioned, he often left the social centre of the Community and spent long spells on his own. Such sojourns could have allowed ambitious males a chance to form a coalition and plot his downfall. On the other hand, since his re-entry into the social centre was uncertain, he came in armed with the element of surprise which any male Kasekelian contemplating rebellion would have found unnerving. Indeed, when he did return, he only had to hint at aggression and that broke the nerve of every potential plotter. Then matters changed unexpectedly.

In the summer of 1997, Freud suffered two mishaps. First, he hurt his foot and developed a limp. He tried to hide this handicap from the other males who would have capitalised on it. But just as his injury was healing, Freud started to lose condition and his hair began to fall out. He became lethargic and couldn't sustain any lengthy physical activity without rest. To avoid being found out, he set off alone deep into the forest. Here he stayed, moving only a little and eating even less. Once, independent-minded Fanni, his younger sister, came across him. She and her baby Fudge stayed with him awhile. She gently groomed him before moving on; Fanni has always been very fond of Freud.

Fanni herself was fit and healthy. So were Frodo, Faustino and many other Kasekelians. But Fifi, her infant Freddi and her son Ferdinand – as well as Titan, Beethoven and several others – were also in a bad way. The afflicted Kasekelians lost a lot of hair and developed white lumps on their skin. The hair loss was accelerated by routine scratching and grooming. In fact, Fifi, Freddi and Ferdinand looked like aliens, having lost all their hair. Although their weird appearance didn't get a second glance from the other Kasekelians, baboons were clearly amazed at their appearance. Once, a troop of baboons passed close to Fifi and Freddi who were resting in shade. They gathered round mother and son, faces curious, eyes popping. They had probably never seen any Kasekelians so weird-looking.

It turned out that the Kasekelians had a virulent form of mange, in which mites burrow into the skin and white lumps appear. Although its cause isn't known and it can be fatal, it isn't usually, and Titan was the first to recover. Once again, he was the energetic, passionately playful, highly inventive juvenile that he had been before being struck down. Ferdinand, too, bounced back. Fifi, who had been so lethargic that she had hardly moved at one stage, also got her strength back, although her recovery was the slowest.

Freddi died. Fifi and Fanni just sat, staring at the dead body. Then Fifi carried the body for days. Freddi was just a kid whose immune system had not fully kicked in. And he may have been weaker than normal because he was the product of mother-son incest. Perhaps a disease is one of nature's ways of eliminating genetic defects in a population responsible for passing on genes.

Freud also inched his way to a full recovery, but before he could regain full strength ambitious males had noticed that something was amiss with him. Despite Freud's exemplary leadership, they were like circling vultures waiting for death to happen. Frodo saw his chance and took it. Freud wasn't in a position to resist and conceded the leadership. Then Frodo did a remarkable thing. He protected Freud, still quite weak, from the young males wanting to assert their dominance over him. This was unusual since leaders that fall tend to be banished or killed straightaway. Perhaps blood is as thick as they say.

Thus Freud relinquished the reins of power. And retirement seemed to become him. He often lay by a stream or a waterfall, lost in thought as he stared at the flowing water. Freud clearly wanted to be left alone, but it wasn't to be. Two young males were keen to rub Freud's nose in his retirement and to dispatch him below themselves in the rankings.

One of them was Gimble, younger brother of Gremlin. When I first set eyes on Gimble in September 2001, it was a cloudy morning. He was examining a fallen palm tree for sustenance and, after a while, started grooming himself. I thought he looked different from the other males but, at first, couldn't pin the difference down. After a while he got up and then I realised that he was quite small and slender.

Gimble was a twin. Gremlin was seven years old when her mother, Melissa, gave birth to Gimble and Gyre. Right from the start, Gyre was the weaker and, as their mother struggled to provide enough milk for both babies, Gimble managed to take a bigger share. At 10 months Gyre caught a respiratory infection and died. From then on Gimble developed fast, as if making up for lost time. However, he remained small for his age right into adulthood.

The other male keen to bully Freud was Tubbe. I don't remember much about him as he was then. Whenever I encountered him, I found him alone. He was the only member of the B dynasty left in Kasekela. His mother had died and his younger sister had migrated to the Mitumba Community in the north. It seemed to me that 24-year-old Tubbe was a quiet soul, content with his own company. However, at the time Frodo had taken over from Freud, Tubbe, then 20, was rising fast in the male hierarchy. He also had hot blood flowing through his brain and he focussed his energies on Freud.

The showdown came early one morning when Freud was quietly feeding in a tree. Tubbe and Gimble climbed up, determined to harass Freud. But the former leader just kept feeding, ignoring the two. Freud, it must be said, is pretty cool and is hardly ever bothered by intimidation. Tubbe and Gimble hesitated in the face of Freud's nonchalance, and Freud continued to feed casually while the pair sat bemused below. Breakfast over, Freud calmly climbed down and sat on the ground some distance from the tree. There he worked himself up into a state of excitement and charged at the young males who promptly turned tail. They had picked on the wrong guy. After that, Freud was able to put all the rest of the hotheads in their place. Yet he didn't seem to hunger for the top spot. He could have wrested it back from Frodo had he tried, but he probably couldn't have cared less.

In the meantime, the male hierarchy under Frodo became very fluid. The old guard such as former leaders Goblin and Wilkie weren't ambitious, merely keen to keep on good terms with Frodo. Tubbe and Gimble were licking their wounds, figuratively speaking. All the other young males, such as Sheldon, Apollo and Kris, were too frightened to upset Frodo, who was steadily tightening his grip at the top.

I had related all this to Fiona years later, in that June of 2011, and she was quite captivated by the story of the brothers, Freud and Frodo. Having already seen and sat with Freud, I was keen for her to meet Frodo.

One morning we started to climb to an area called Bald Soko, a large expanse of tall grass interspersed with a few trees covering the slopes higher up. To reach it, we followed a trail that wound up a forested slope. Below us at the edge of Bald Soko, the ground fell away towards the blue-grey expanse of Lake Tanganyika. Lines and patches of green, starting just below the smooth, golden-brown humps and ridges of the dry upper slopes, gradually became darker and thicker as they descended and then converged as they followed the maze of gullies and ravines that led down to the thickly forested valleys. To the north and south, valley succeeded valley, each leading its own swift-flowing stream westward, from the watershed, high in the hills, down to the lake.

Unexpectedly, we bumped into Frodo, feeding. I immediately recognised him by his face, but his body shape looked different. My memory of the Frodo of ten or so years earlier was of a big, strong, assertive male. The Frodo before us was leaner and grizzled.

We learned that Frodo had become a loner. Occasionally an adolescent male would accompany him and Frodo would tolerate the youngster as long as he received grooming. This was so like the old Frodo, to receive grooming but rarely to groom back. There was one change in that Frodo had lost his appetite for flexing his muscles. His appetite for food remained unchanged, though – he still ate prodigious amounts. Back at the rest-house, I remembered Frodo as he was a decade earlier and all that had happened to him since then.

Big and powerful, highly intelligent and utterly confident, Frodo had looked set for a long reign. He had just one problem, a social one: except for Goblin, no other male wanted his company. The young upstarts were terrified of him and the old guard preferred to keep their distance. Frodo's situation was akin to many classroom bullies with no genuine friends, only a yes-man or two. In his loneliness Frodo eagerly sought Freud's company. The problem was Frodo wanted both to dominate Freud and to have him as a companion.

Freud had other ideas. He was quite prepared to acknowledge Frodo as the leader, but not to have friendship imposed on him. So despite Frodo's entreaties and much to his disappointment, Freud firmly stuck to his solitary ways. Frodo did have Goblin, though. Goblin had forsaken Freud and begun to cultivate a friendly relationship with Frodo. In this, there was a clear advantage to Goblin – he couldn't be pushed around.

Consider an incident that occurred one clear October morning during my second visit to the Kasekelians way back in 2001. Goblin was by himself and was then joined by two males, Wilkie and Sheldon. The two displayed at him, sending him screaming to the top of a tree, where he stayed for several minutes. From this vantage he saw Frodo arriving, whereupon he descended and displayed at the two males, who fled. All of the four players knew that Goblin could have successfully called on Frodo if he had needed to. Goblin stayed with Frodo for the rest of the morning, grooming him from time to time, much to Frodo's obvious pleasure.

In the beginning of his reign, Frodo was thoroughly unpopular. Lacking friends and allies apart from Goblin, Frodo had no choice but to rule by terror. So if he got to know of a grooming party of males, he would arrive suddenly and savagely break it up. He played on the others' fears by erupting into sudden rages that terrified all in the vicinity. Whenever he approached a resting group, his entrance was electrifying. The females would head for safety, mothers grabbing their infants in haste. I once saw Apollo, a high-ranking male, quickly carry away a baby that had been blissfully making its way toward Frodo. There was uncertainty in the air, and most Kasekelians simply chose to avoid their leader.

But time can work wonders. As Frodo grew confident that he neither faced any opposition nor was likely to, he relaxed. The Kasekelians sensed this. They also seemed to realise that since Frodo's dominance was absolute, there was less disruption to everyday life because the ambitious males were no longer jockeying for position to challenge him as leader. Most Kasekelians welcomed the respite from the leadership struggle and, as long as someone groomed Frodo, he was unlikely to fly into a temper.

His deliberate substitution of brawn for tact had put off the females, however, and it took them some time to adjust to Frodo as a less disruptive leader. I remember one instance early on in his reign when a group of females was sitting and Frodo arrived alone in a calm state. He solicited grooming but no one obliged. In fact, the group moved a few yards away from him, underscoring a social snub. Frodo was nonplussed and moved on to find someone who would groom him.

Frodo, of course, wasn't one to be deterred by social snubs. He believed he had prior rights to mate with any female, and woe betide any female who should refuse him. In addition, Frodo was intolerant of any male consorting with a female. Consider the time when a group had climbed high up a hill and Frodo had been left behind. Fanni was in that group and proving irresistible to the group's males. When Frodo caught up and saw the males surrounding Fanni, he lost his temper. He careered through them and beat the daylights out of one who had been slow to get lost. It was a brutal, terrifying performance. But I suspect it was also a well calculated one. When all is said and done, he did sire more offspring than any Kasekelian leader, except Wilkie, for several generations.

Frodo wasn't only the leader; he was also the top hunter. He wasn't intimidated by male colobus monkeys that gallantly and fiercely defend females with young when the Kasekelians target them. I saw Frodo use his enormous strength to climb trees quickly, cutting-off escape routes of the targeted monkeys with greater success than the other Kasekelians. It's on record that during one dry season he caught 20 monkeys.

Sheldon is also an excellent hunter. I first caught a glimpse of him when he was 18 years old, on a cloudy September day in 2001 in the cool Kakombe valley. The males had heard cries of monkeys in trees and had begun hunting. Ten males had leapt into the trees in a successful bid to drive the panic-stricken monkeys to tall isolated trees and then pick them off. They caught four that morning. Sheldon walked by me with a partially-eaten monkey and disappeared with his prize.

Sheldon hails from the large S dynasty which is ranked below the F dynasty. He had and still has a powerful build, and he often revealed bravery beyond his years. As a result, he moved quite quickly up the male hierarchy. But Sheldon had one problem – poor self-belief. He lacked confidence when dealing with the males from the F dynasty. In fact, he was so respectful of Frodo that it would never have crossed his mind to challenge him for the leadership.

It was on an afternoon in September 2001 that Sheldon once again displayed his hunting skills. There was a cool breeze blowing that afternoon which made climbing less arduous than usual. The Kasekelians had come across a tiny patch of tall grass and Sheldon was the first to detect a bushbuck fawn lying still in it. He stalked it silently, grabbed it before it could make a bid for freedom and then carried the crying fawn up a tree. Frodo, who had been slower off the mark, caught up with Sheldon. This was a dilemma for Sheldon who was nervous about Frodo but wanted to keep his prize. Frodo, though, being Frodo, was decisive. He grabbed the fawn from Sheldon's hand and then knocked him off the tree. Sheldon retired, but a noisy group of Kasekelians gathered around Frodo, each one utterly absorbed in watching Frodo with the kill but also wanting a share. However, until he had had his fill, Frodo wasn't ready to share. He gripped the carcass tightly in his mouth and, with hair bristling, displayed, sending a clear message to the gathering that he was in command.

Half an hour later, having satisfied his yearning for flesh, Frodo gave Goblin a leg and began to reward the persistent beggars, perhaps to buy some peace and quiet. Fifi, who had been sitting quietly, didn't get anything from her son and Goblin didn't bother to share at all.

While Frodo was number one in the hierarchy and the top hunter, he wasn't the best of leaders. One of a leader's tasks is to initiate and lead territorial patrols. To the north of Kasekela is the hostile Mitumba Community and to the South is the small Kalande Community. Border encroachments occur, and relations between the Communities are tense. It's built into their psyches to secure and expand territories, hence the need for border patrols. When they were leaders, Goblin, Wilkie

and Freud led such patrols. Frodo, however, couldn't be bothered, and so the task fell on, of all the Kasekelians, Pax.

I had first encountered Pax – he was 24 years old then – on a bright, clear, morning during my second visit to Kasekela in 2001. The Kasekelians were moving through a more open patch of the forest strewn with large rocks. The insignificant figure of Pax was bringing up the rear. This was, and still is, his mode of operation: to stay at the fringes of a group. He will, however, join the males whenever they request grooming from him. He himself does not receive any grooming from any of the males. Without doubt, he is the lowest-ranking male in the Community.

Pax is impotent. A wound suffered when he was three years old from an attack by the Kalande Community to the south resulted in him losing both of his testicles. So he never reached puberty. (Pax's mother died when he was four, and he was subsequently cared for by his older sister Pom and older brother Prof.) He has never been strong or big and from a distance can be mistaken for a female. Since he also mixes well with the Community youngsters, he could be called Kasekela's Peter Pan.

Pax has a couple of prized abilities: one is that he is very good at locating fruiting trees and, whenever he is noticed leaving a group, the others follow. He can also lead a territorial patrol, making skilful use of his knowledge of the terrain at the borders. There was one memorable occasion when he led a patrol to the south. It was a silent march with frequent stops to look and scan for the enemy. At the border, a young Kalendian was spotted in a tree. He tried to get away but the Kasekelian males were quick to surround the tree and cut off all escape routes. He was caught and beaten. A hyped-up Frodo was particularly brutal, jumping on the prone victim several times with the full force of his 55kg frame. When the victim fell into a stream, Frodo abruptly stopped his savage attack and the Kasekelians let off steam by hugging each other and displaying all over the scene of the violence. Then they returned to the north, leaving the victim in the stream. After some time, he slowly hauled himself out and painfully made his way south.

On my third visit to The Kasekela Community in late 2002, I discovered that 44-year-old Fifi was close to giving birth. Normally a social being, Fifi had temporarily turned reclusive. Only her daughter, four-year-old Flirt, accompanied her everywhere. Fifi also rested a lot, much to Flirt's incomprehension and disappointment. Flirt was clearly bored and whiled away time grooming Fifi – quite reminiscent of the time when Fifi's mother, Flo, was pregnant and a juvenile Fifi used to groom her for long periods.

The indomitable Fifi spent the last day of her pregnancy climbing steep slopes and descending into deep valleys before resting for the night. The next day, she was a mother again. The birth of Furaha, as the newborn was named, had been uneventful, unlike the day Flirt had been born more than four years earlier.

Flirt was Fifi's eighth baby and after her birth Fifi had lain on the ground, one hand pinning Flirt to her chest, the other holding placenta which she ate leisurely and with obvious relish. Perhaps it was the smell that soon attracted a small crowd of baboons, including a couple of males baring their large canine teeth. Determined and fearless, the baboons inched closer and closer until they were within touching distance of Fifi, who had been calmly watching them all the time. She looked at the aggressive males from her reclining position and contemplated her predicament. It was typical of her to be unhurried even when faced with such a tricky situation. Fifi didn't want to give up her placenta, and she wanted to eat it in peace. She sat up, lunged at the baboons and, having created space, walked away. The baboons pursued her. She broke into a run and climbed a tree so that she could defend her position from the baboons gathered below. Then she resumed her leisurely feeding. Once she finished the food, the baboons scattered. Fifi climbed down and walked away casually, holding new-born Flirt to her chest. She rested in a sheltered spot in the forest and was presently joined by her two sons, Ferdinand and Faustino. They were intensely curious about the new arrival in the family – a big baby with large eyes. Big size seems to run in the F dynasty.

Fanni, too, turned up carrying Fudge. Eighteen-month-old Fudge was fascinated by Flirt and was irresistibly drawn to touch her. Although he was apprehensive of the watchful Fifi, he did manage to touch Flirt's legs, an act which Fifi studiously ignored. Then someone else was approaching Fifi. She sat up, alert. It was Frodo and it was wise to be ready to flee when her son was around. Frodo had been in power for nine months and was still inclined to throw his weight around. Frodo came to Fifi and looked at his new sister. Flirt seemed to fascinate him and also exert a calming effect on him as he watched her. It turned out to be the beginning of a long-term bond between them.

Now, four years later, a baby girl, Furaha, was the latest addition to the F Dynasty. After birth, Fifi continued her solitary ways for a few more days. Perhaps she wanted to be away from the social hurly-burly of a group, especially with its excitable and unpredictable males and boisterous youngsters. When the rest of the F family finally found her, the boys – especially Ferdinand and Faustino – became extremely protective of Fifi and Furaha.

On my fourth visit to Kasekela Community one year later, I found that Fifi and Furaha were doing well, although Fifi had her hands full looking after both Flirt and Furaha. On one occasion, Flirt got frightened and cried, refusing to follow Fifi. So Fifi turned back and carried both of them until Flirt was more at ease. Flirt's crying, though, was a sign that she wasn't happy to be receiving less attention from her mother as a result of Furaha's arrival. But then, the 45-year-old matriarch of Kasekela was getting old. She was content to lie down after feeding, clutching Furaha to her chest, leaving Flirt to amuse herself.

When I left the Kasekelians toward the end of the dry season of 2002, things appeared settled. Frodo had become less intimidating now that he felt secure as leader, even though he did put the occasional boot in to remind everyone of his absolute authority. He was set to become a long-term autocrat who was bad for democracy but good for stability. Freud, fully fit and still very powerful, had settled into an idyllic retirement. The F dynasty was entrenched in a dominant position. But matters were about to change.

Frodo feeding in a palm tree in Kakombe valley. The Kasekelians are agile and well adapted to their forest home. It is with enviable ease that they get around in the dense thickets down in the valleys and up the slopes. To keep up with them when they are on the move, you need to contort your body in many different ways, and to persevere you have to listen to your inner voice, ignoring the ambushes of vines, shrubs, thorns and holes the forest lays down.

Then: Frodo. 26-year-old Frodo knew one thing
for sure – he had the physique and the power that
goes with it. Being smart, he used it to climb to the
very top of the male hierarchy.

Now: 36-year-old Frodo. Ten years later he could be considered a wise statesman of Kasekela, uninterested in the battle for leadership but happy to be involved in the affairs of the Community. There was one noticeable change in Frodo: back then he used to lack social finesse; ten years on he was a little more considerate.

Then: 31-year-old Freud being groomed by a male. Despite having lost the leadership about four years earlier, he remained a high-ranking male and a force to be reckoned with. Freud wasn't particularly big, but he could give an illusion of power with electrifying displays that left his audience stunned. After Frodo fell ill and had to relinquish power, Freud could have become the leader again, but his heart wasn't in it. Once was enough.

Now: 41-year-old Freud. He is the oldest Kasekelian male alive today. His face looks slightly battered, and his nose is markedly misshapen – scars of a life lived. He rarely displays now, content to live on the political margins. He commands a great deal of respect and affection, though. Once, when he unexpectedly appeared, all the F family members – adults and young ones – went to him either to groom him or to sit next to him, and I could see the quiet satisfaction in his eyes and posture.

Then: 24-year-old Tubbe. He was content with his own company. His mother had died and his only other relative, younger sister Darbee, had migrated to the adjoining Mitumba Community to the north. He wasn't always uninterested in social affairs. When he was between 18 and 21, he was quite aggressive about climbing the male hierarchy. Then, inexplicably, he gave up on his ambition.

Then: 25-year-old Gimble, younger brother of Gremlin.
Gimble and Gyre were twins, but right from birth,
even though Gimble was small, Gyre was the weaker.
Moreover, by taking a larger share of their mother's
milk, Gimble denied Gyre a chance to catch up with
him. Then, at ten months of age, Gyre caught a
respiratory infection and died.

A line of Kasekelians traversing the open grassy stretch of Bald Soko. They are on their way to a fruiting tree higher up the Rift Valley escarpment. Below Bald Soko, the forest begins at the shore of Lake Tanganyika and covers the lower slopes all the way to Bald Soko. Above there, the forest thins out quite quickly.

Frodo, when I saw him again after a gap of 10 years. The giant of the past looked no bigger than any of the other adult males. He had also become irrelevant as a male influence. Often we would find him alone or with a juvenile whom he treated as a grooming slave in exchange for the privilege of being tolerated by the great Frodo.

Frodo, ten years on. Though he was no longer competing for the leadership, I would sometimes search Frodo's face and see that he still had that life-force in the spark of his eyes.

Frodo holding a bushbuck fawn as Goblin gestures to
Fifi to keep away from the meat. It was Sheldon who
had caught the fawn and gone up the tree with it. Frodo
quickly followed, grabbed the fawn and at the same
time knocked Sheldon off the tree. From then on, Frodo
controlled the situation. He gave a large share to Goblin
but otherwise refused to share until he had had enough.

Kasekelians gathering around Ferdinand. He is in command of a colobus monkey carcass, and they hope to get a share of the meat. Little Zinda is right up there, already rewarded with a share. Zinda's mother, Zrezia, is coaxing her son to share with her. Sparrow, who loves meat, is begging persistently. Ferdinand, in total command of the situation, is deliberately ignoring Titan, standing. Titan probably knows that he is unlikely to get anything, but that doesn't stop him from trying.

Then: 19-year-old Sheldon, an expert hunter. Here he carries a red colobus monkey to a secluded place away from other Kasekelians who would surely pester him for a share. Sheldon then was a risk-taker, chancing a fall when chasing after monkeys in treetops. As a hunter, he was second only to Frodo.

Now: 29-year-old Sheldon is the eldest of Sparrow's boys. Impressive physically, Sheldon comes across as someone who is hard to know mentally. He identifies closely with his family, quite happy to look after his mother Sparrow and younger brother Sinbad. Once, when Sheldon came back after a long absence, an overjoyed Sinbad ran for more than a 100 metres to greet him.

Then: 24-year-old Pax. A wound to his groin caused when he was about three years old by an attack from the males of the Kalande Community resulted in his never reaching puberty and in his permanent impotence. A year after the injury, Pax's mother died and he was subsequently looked after by his elder brother and sister.

Now: 34-year-old Pax. He is neither big nor strong, and he is, not surprisingly, the lowest-ranking male in Kasekela. He generally keeps out of the way of the adult males and only joins them to groom them when he senses that they are in a benign mood. He mixes well with the young in the Community and can be thought of as 'the Peter Pan of Kasekela'. In fact, over the course of Pax's life, several orphans have attached themselves to him.

Fifi, 44, then the dominant matriarch at Kasekela. She rests
in shady thicket with her two-day-old baby girl, Furaha. I
was with Fifi for a few days before and after Furaha's birth.
It was difficult to keep up with Fifi then as she went down
steep valleys, up sharp inclines and climbed tall trees
seemingly effortlessly. It was hard to take in that she was
an old lady.

Fifi with one-year-old Furaha. By the time she was 45, Fifi had given birth to nine offspring, only one of which, Freddi, had not survived. One of her daughters, Flossi, had established herself in Mitumba Community and was already a mother of two. Her eldest daughter, Fanni, had stayed on in Kasekela and was also a mother of two. Her eldest son, Freud, had been a leader, and her second eldest son, Frodo, was the then leader. In short, Fifi could look back on a successful life.

Chapter 3: **The Struggle for Power**

Towards the end of 2002, there was an ailment in the Community that weakened many Kasekelians. Most lost weight, particularly Frodo, Goblin, Kris and Apollo.

Then another ailment struck soon afterwards in December. Frodo started suffering from a disease of parasites in his stomach that weakened him considerably. He took off to a hiding place in the forest and lay his body down. Too weak to move, he stayed there for several days. When slow recovery kicked in, he moved a little, trying to keep away from others, especially the males who would have capitalised on his weakness.

It turned out that the males had, in fact, noticed Frodo's absence and could sense that it was unusual. Perhaps there was now the possibility of challenging him for the leadership. So began their posturing and strutting as each one plotted a path to the top. One of the contenders was Apollo.

My earliest memory of Apollo is from the very first visit I made to Gombe. I was walking on a forest trail covered with dry, crunchy leaves, and there, in a tiny clearing next to the trail, was 22-year-old Apollo, sitting regally on a tree buttress. He seemed to be listening for a call. After a silence lasting a few minutes, he kicked repeatedly on the tree buttress, producing an impressive drumming sound which carried far and wide. When he heard a reply, he went towards its source and disappeared from view.

Apollo then was without any relatives, his mother, Athena, having passed away when he was quite young. By sheer determination he had climbed so far up the male hierarchy that, at the time of Frodo's temporary absence, he was a high-ranking male and appeared to be the keenest to take a shot at the leadership. Actually, he had wanted to be the leader since the age of 14 but had been thwarted by Fifi's boys, first Freud and then Frodo. Now he appeared to have another chance. To

bolster his bid, he tried to strike up an alliance with the former leader, Goblin. However, Goblin, while friendly with Apollo, was too canny to commit himself. He wanted to ally himself with the best candidate and it wasn't clear to him whether Apollo had it in him to be the frontrunner. So, since Goblin preferred to keep his options open, Apollo couldn't count on him.

The situation, as Goblin saw it, was that the muscular Sheldon was the one to beat and that Apollo was reluctant to take him on. Sheldon was at an age, 20, when young males take risks. He also had a family behind him. He was the eldest male in the maternal S dynasty started by Sparrow. Most of the time, her well-knit dynasty kept away from the rest of the Kasekela Community, where the F dynasty was treated like royalty. However, with hot blood nourishing his brain, Sheldon was spending more time in the centre of the Community than any other member of the S dynasty.

Also in the running was Gimble. Since neither he nor Apollo dared to take Sheldon on singly, they tried to build an alliance. There was a problem, though. While Apollo and Gimble shared an interest in dominating Sheldon (and any other candidate for the leadership), they were also in conflict in that each wanted to be sole leader. Then something happened to wreck their negotiations. Apollo grew progressively weaker. He seemed to be infected with the same parasite that had laid Frodo low. Ever the opportunist, Gimble saw a chance to reduce the number of contestants and turned on Apollo, picking on his former friend to such an extent that Apollo went into temporary exile and dropped out of the leadership race.

Kris, the sole surviving member of the K family, was also in the running. He had also been infected by the stomach parasite but was making a steady recovery. Unlike the excitable Apollo, Kris was by nature relaxed and could take the long view. He had worked out that, even if fully fit, he would find it very difficult to defeat Sheldon on his own. Moreover, unlike Sheldon, he did not have family support. Yet he sensed that Sheldon lacked something a leader should possess: confidence. He could see that in the hesitancy and indecisiveness that surfaced in Sheldon at times. So Kris settled down and waited, politely turning down overtures from potential allies. He was a nice guy, but he wanted the leadership for himself.

The dark horse for the leadership was Freud. It was only when he had fallen ill that he'd had to give up the leadership to his heavyweight brother, Frodo. Now that Frodo was absent, Freud must have looked around and thought that he was in with a chance himself.

All the contenders respected Freud, with his astute mind and vast experience, but none seemed to want to ally with him. The reason wasn't difficult to spot. When Freud had relinquished power, the young upstarts had tried to dominate him but Freud had taken them on and dispatched them with his terrifying displays. When he chose to, Freud could work himself up into a frenzied mood, breaking and swinging branches and kicking up fallen leaves and debris. For a young, ambitious male to ally with such a powerful personality would have meant playing second fiddle, and that wasn't agreeable to any of them.

Freud, for his part, had no wish to ally himself with any of them, least of all Goblin. Quite simply, he didn't trust Goblin. He remembered how Goblin had changed allegiance when Freud was defending his leadership from Frodo's challenge. Goblin was too Machiavellian, too unreliable. He could abandon you in your hour of need.

Wilkie, another old guard and former leader, was a possibility. After all, Freud had been instrumental in allowing him – after a long, lonely spell in exile – to re-enter the social life of the Community. Those had been tough days for Wilkie. So Freud had substantial credit with Wilkie for facilitating his re-integration. There was a niggle in Freud's mind, though: he could sense that Wilkie's heart wasn't in it. Wilkie was content with a quiet life. Though well respected, he was now without ambition. And without Wilkie's firm commitment there was no point in allying with him.

Freud would have to go it alone. He had it in him to be the leader again, but it wasn't clear whether he was prepared to work very hard for the position. After all, he was happy in his retirement, would need drive and energy to engage in a long campaign and would have to take his gloves off if he was serious. Then something happened involving Frodo.

Frodo's recovery had been proceeding slowly but steadily. He was still in hiding, though, still on his own, still a fugitive when Sheldon chanced upon him in early January 2003. In the past, Sheldon would have quickly acknowledged Frodo's superior status, but this time Sheldon was feeling very confident and Frodo, aware of his weakened state, was nervous. All the Kasekelians are ultra-quick to read a situation, and Sheldon noticed Frodo's hesitancy straight away. So, under Sheldon's critical eye, Frodo's nerve broke and he grovelled before him. Astonished but pleased nevertheless, Sheldon accepted Frodo's acknowledge-

ment of his superiority, and so matters stood when they went their separate ways. However, Frodo was far from being reintegrated into the Community, as a dramatic incident a couple of weeks later demonstrated. The day began uneventfully, as it usually does in this land, but then, later on, the quiet of the forest was punctuated by a loud cacophony. There was a quick flurry of activity in the treetops and then stillness. But the calm lasted for only a few minutes before bedlam broke out. Working as a team, a few males had managed to catch a colobus monkey and were, as could be expected, audibly excited. In fact, no other sound could be heard over the Kasekelians screaming and calling at the tops of their voices. In addition to the noise, the males ran everywhere, hugging and kissing each other. Those that were begging for a share of the meat were set upon by the high-ranking males in possession of it. There were cries and screams from the ones who were beaten for their temerity, and the sounds carried far in the stillness of the air. Frodo, being in the vicinity, heard them.

Frodo knew what the noise meant – it was too distinctive to mean anything else. In fact, he had heard it many, many times before and, for that matter, had often been involved in many such successful hunts. The noises he heard stirred his longing for flesh. And he was torn. He was stronger than when he had fallen ill but he still had some way to go to regain full fitness. He had now been alone, save for the brief encounter with Sheldon, for two interminably long months. He couldn't predict how a gathering of males would receive him. On the other hand, there was the possibility of getting his hands on the meat his body was craving for.

Frodo wasn't thinking straight. He should have taken into account the heightened state of excitement of the males. Anyone encroaching on their highly charged party, let alone a hated former dictator, would most likely be met with hostility and violence. If Frodo were to walk into the feeding frenzy, he'd have to be careful with his body language. If he betrayed even the slightest hint of nervousness, the males would have no hesitation in going for him.

Torn between good sense and a craving for meat, his stomach won and Frodo walked into the melee. The males stared for a split second; after all, none of them had seen him for a long time apart from Sheldon. Then the males tore into Frodo without restraint. But in the confusion of the mauling, he had a lucky break and escaped. The males chased him half-heartedly – after all, they had meat on their minds – and he managed to avoid a serious beating. Though he had saved his skin, paradoxically, being so close to the others sowed the seed in his brain to belong to the Community again.

So he tried to ingratiate himself back into the group, and the pull to be with his kind took on an irresistible force for him. But all the males had got wise to his nervousness and took him on. Frodo tried meekness and sent out every signal of submission he could think of. It was to no avail. Life became hell for Frodo and this manifested itself through his weight loss and his nervous disposition. Such was his anxiety that whenever young Faustino displayed to impress the females, and even though the displays weren't directed at Frodo, Frodo would

scream. He was a nervous wreck and couldn't take it any more. So Frodo went back into exile.

Even in exile, Frodo was jumpy. His only hope was to be with someone who wouldn't make him nervous – and that was Freud. He finally tracked Freud down and stayed with him whenever he could. Encouraged, he then mixed with the others from the F dynasty. That helped both to bolster his confidence and to shield him from pot shots from any passing males. Gradually the males realised that Frodo was staying on and also that he wasn't a threat to their rankings. So, little by little, Frodo was able to settle into a peripheral role, quite like that of Pax, uninvolved in male politics. He also made sure that he paid his respects to the likes of Sheldon, Gimble and Kris – a vivid illustration of how far he had fallen.

Meanwhile Sheldon was emerging as the front runner for the leadership. One by one, the obstacles in his path to the top were disappearing. Gimble, who was frail in comparison with Sheldon, was losing condition slowly. He could also see that Sheldon's star was in ascendancy. So he gave up his bid for leadership by acknowledging that Sheldon was indeed of higher rank than him. By June 2003, only Freud and Kris stood in Sheldon's way.

Freud was having second thoughts too. He realised that he couldn't bring himself to conduct a long campaign. He had the brains to outmanoeuvre Sheldon and Kris but not the inclination. His hunger for the leadership wasn't acute enough; retirement suited his temperament more. He decided that he was quite content to be a high-ranking male and left it at that.

That left Sheldon and Kris. Had Kris fully recovered from the parasite infection, he would have been an even match for Sheldon. As matters stood, Sheldon had both the edge in physical combat and the S dynasty behind him. In any case, it wasn't in Kris's nature to take unnecessary risks. He was a patient guy, wise in his ways, prepared to wait, filling his time by studying Sheldon's strengths and weaknesses. Thus Sheldon stumbled into the leadership without opposition, with both Kris and Freud at joint number two.

At the beginning of Sheldon's tenure as leader, the Community was unsettled, perhaps because Sheldon's personality wasn't conducive to stability. He wasn't cool, calm or confident. He was aware of his shortcomings and was tempted, at times, to chuck it in. However, it wasn't easy to relinquish the heady feeling of power. He was torn between a quiet life without power and a tense life with it – torn between his personal inclinations and the conspiracy of circumstances. His inner conflict couldn't last. Kris noticed, watched and readied himself.

In a habitat that features steep slopes, precipitous ravines, tall grass and thickets that seem impenetrable, the Kasekelians are much more competent at navigation then I am or ever could be.

Then: Apollo. I first came across 22-year-old
Apollo sitting on a tree buttress. He was waiting
to connect with the other males, from whom,
seemingly, he had lost contact. Apollo then had
no family. His only relative, his mother Athena, had
died a long time ago, but by sheer determination
he had climbed up the male hierarchy.

Now: 32-year-old Apollo. He was often in the company of high-ranking males, roaming with them, grooming them and receiving grooming in turn. In the past, Apollo had had his sights set on the leadership but he had been thwarted, first by Freud and then by Frodo. He couldn't bring himself to challenge either when they were leaders. Subsequently, he descended rapidly down the male hierarchy.

Then: 44-year-old Sparrow. Sparrow may have immigrated to Kasekela, but no one knows for sure. She was aloof then, keeping herself and her family secluded, except when she was sexually receptive.

Now: 55-year-old Sparrow. Sparrow today is the oldest living Kasekelian. She doesn't have any apparent physical ailments. She looks younger than her age and is physically active, travelling long distances, keeping up with fast-moving males and climbing tall trees with ease.

Tubbe, 24, was once a high-ranking male but quickly dropped down the rankings. He took to frequenting the southern edge of the Community, not coming into contact with high-ranking males for long periods of time. It was as if he had made a conscious decision to retire from the heat of mainstream politics.

Kris, 20, was the only survivor from the K dynasty. A marked characteristic of Kris was that he wasn't easily excited, taking his time to work things out calmly before acting. My memory of him is of a quiet, likeable soul.

Chapter 4: **Kris, Fanni and Others**

The end to Sheldon's inner conflict at being leader was an anticlimax. There was no showdown. One fine day in the middle of 2004, Sheldon quietly left the centre of the group – he had had enough. The others noticed the vacuum in due course and also noticed Kris stepping in to fill it. No one challenged him. There was no struggle for power, no acrimonious disputes. Instead, all the males, including Freud and Gimble, acknowledged him as the new leader. Freud was now too settled in his comfortable niche and Gimble had become physically weaker.

So there was just a resigned acceptance of change at the top. It was as if the Community members wanted to get on with the task of living their lives in an atmosphere of calm. Kris's triumph, accomplished with patience, seemed complete. Then, six months later, from his self-imposed exile on the periphery, Sheldon unexpectedly turned up in the heart of the Community. He had found the exile difficult and yearned for social stimulus. But as a returning former leader, he was risking the wrath of the other males, especially Kris.

Sheldon was no fool. He was aware of the possible reaction of the males and he had a plan. He had worked out that Kris was now the undisputed leader and he knew Kris to be good-natured. So Sheldon went straight to him, paid his respects and waited nervously for Kris to respond. Kris had no quarrel with Sheldon as long as Sheldon had no designs on the leadership and, as Sheldon grovelled before him, Kris sensed that this was the case. So Kris was forgiving and Sheldon was back in the fold. Unfortunately for Kris, while his assessment of Sheldon had been spot on, he had neglected to look over his shoulder – for a challenge did come and it appeared from an unexpected quarter. In the meantime, with the onset of rains in November, the year was drawing to a close and Kris appeared well in command.

Meanwhile, a word about two significant deaths in 2004.

It was in August or September that Fifi disappeared with her two-year-old daughter, Furaha. Fifi had taken to ranging near the turf of the Mitumba Community, far from her normal range in the Kasekela's centre. It wasn't in Fifi's character or style to forsake her bountiful normal range and go wandering off. There was no apparent compulsion, no obvious need. Even at 46, Fifi looked fit and healthy, without any signs of disability, discomfort or illness. She still had a few good years left in her. Yet on 17 September six-year-old Flirt was seen wandering in the forest alone and Fifi and Furaha were never seen again. How come? Could it be that she was set upon by the Mitumba Community with fatal consequences? If so, it would have been a traumatic experience for Flirt.

The years following Fifi's disappearance were tough for Flirt. Fortunately for her, she was befriended by an old female called Candy. Frodo, too, helped Flirt whenever he was around. He was still rehabilitating himself in the Community and was prone to avoiding young males. In fact, this was the start of his carving out a niche for himself as a strong senior citizen. Flirt's other brothers also played their part in looking after her. For a time she appeared depressed and stopped playing. But she hung on nevertheless and, within two to three years of Fifi's death, she was fine again, healthy and playing with little kids whenever she was in a group. It was also clear that she preferred to be on her own, and she seemed to relish her independence.

That year Goblin also succumbed to a fatal illness. On 7 August he was seen moving very slowly, unable to scale trees and eating very little. He continued like this until 18 August. On that afternoon, a fast-moving wall of fire appeared on the eastern hills and, fuelled by strong winds, it spread to feed on the trees and undergrowth of the 12 valleys. Although Goblin survived the fire, which burned for nearly a week more, he died when his heart stopped beating on 24 August. A post-mortem examination indicated that he had been suffering from a high intestinal parasite load. He was 40 years old. A small part of local history died with him, but his genes lived on in Tom and Tabora (via Tanga) and Fudge, Fundi, Fadhila and Fifty (via Fanni).

When he was the undisputed leader, Goblin had been a possessive, jealous suitor, and males gave a wide berth to the females in his sights. One of these was Tatti, who was large and seemed to have had a thing for macho males – namely, Goblin and Frodo. Anyway, Goblin and Tatti begat Tanga who now has a child called Tom.

Goblin also managed, by sheer persistence, to mate with Fifi. Fanni was the outcome which bodes well for Goblin's genes because Fanni takes after Fifi as far as rapid and successful reproduction goes. As matters stood in 2013, Fanni had given birth to six children and, being only 30 years old, was likely to have a few more. Indeed, overall, Goblin has done well if you consider the principal dynasties at Kasekela. If we follow matrilineal lines they are the F, G, S and T dynasties and Goblin's genes are present in a significant way in three out of the four.

I had told Fiona about Goblin and his legacy and, during her first visit to Kasekela in June 2011, she was keen to meet Fanni. In typical Fanni fashion she had taken to ranging away from the centre of the Community and proved hard to find. We heard that she regularly had three kids in tow, sometimes four, and occasionally even five. We kept on trying and then one day we got lucky.

It was a calm morning when we started out, and I remember that the lake was very still. As we climbed, it looked emerald all the way to Congo and Burundi. We found Fanni and it was deja vu. We had seen a film clip of Fanni when she was about a year old, and the sight that greeted us that day – Fanni with her nine-month-old baby boy, Fifty – was as if Fanni was carrying herself, so remarkable was the likeness between baby Fifty and Fanni when at the same age.

Fiona and I spent the entire pleasant morning with Fanni. It seemed uncannily similar to the times I had spent with her a decade or so earlier. At midday, when the sun was bright above us and the sounds of the forest had quietened down, Fanni rested in shade on the ground. She lay prone with one eye on her kids playing, ignoring our presence totally.

We met up with Fanni and her three children quite regularly after that day. Fanni's persona has not changed much. She still sits, seemingly lost in thought, wearing her characteristic glazed expression, staring into nothing. Also, when resting lying down, she still puts her hand on her forehead, as if some small detail is weighing on her mind. It's clear to me that Fanni is determined to live her life her way. She certainly doesn't appear to be bothered by rank. Headstrong, she is her own boss.

And she seems to have matured as a mother. In the same year that Fifi and Goblin died, their genes, which came together in Fanni, carried on when Fanni delivered Familia. Familia is four years younger than her brother Fundi, who in turn is three years younger than his brother Fudge. For a period after Familia's birth, all three siblings stayed together with Fanni. The interesting thing about the three is that they are full siblings, that is, they have the same mother and father – the father being Sheldon.

Sheldon sired Familia when he was the ambivalent leader, but it seems that there had always been something deeper going on between him and Fanni. Perhaps the driving force was Fanni exercising choice. Like her mother, she didn't migrate. She stayed on in Kasekela, surrounded by figures she was related to and others she was acquainted with. She wisely avoided her brothers in matters of sex. She similarly avoided her father, Goblin, and her uncle, Gimble. That meant that her set of acceptable suitors was small – Apollo, Wilkie, Tubbe, Beethoven, Kris and Sheldon.

And she first chose Sheldon. As far as I can tell from the records, Sheldon has not sired any other offspring apart from Fanni's first three children. Of course he might have, and the babies might have died very soon after birth – you can't be certain. Nevertheless, I believe there was some very strong attraction between Sheldon and Fanni, and that resulted in Fudge, Fundi and Familia. But if Fanni and other females are able to exercise choice, then it makes you wonder what is the point, for a male, of being the leader? After all, being at the top of the male hierarchy is stressful and fraught with uncertainty. If exclusive access to the females isn't the compensating pay-off, I wonder what is.

The relationship between Fanni and Sheldon was reminiscent of the one between Sandi and Apollo. Sandi is Sheldon's elder sister. In her youth she was very close to her mother, Sparrow. She was also quite nervous around groups but relaxed if either Sparrow or Apollo was around. Not surprisingly, Sandi and Apollo eventually courted and mated, and Sampson was the result. Incidentally, when Sampson was an infant, Sandi was very reluctant to let him mix with the other Kasekelians. Over time, though, she relaxed and let him interact, which Sampson did with delight and glee, and you could often see him in the thick of things.

The other child of Sandi and Apollo is Siri. Both Sampson and Siri have inherited Apollo's distinctive bright orange eyes, just as Titan and Tarzan have inherited Frodo's size.

Fanni and Sheldon, Sandi and Apollo, Frodo and Tatti (father and mother of both Titan and Tarzan) – all, as couples, were intimate over long periods of time. They would often slip away to spend private quality time together. They weren't always undisturbed, though. Once, when Frodo and Tatti sneaked off yet again, Tarzan, a mere kid, tagged along. They went near the border of Kasekela and Mitumba communities, hoping for a spell of tranquillity, but it was not to be. No one knows exactly what happened that day. It seems that a Mitumba male patrol spotted the three of them. Maybe the patrol had crept silently upon the Kasekelians, caught them unaware and attacked. Frodo and Tarzan escaped – 44-year-old Tatti didn't. She was probably slower to flee and, enraged at Frodo's presence, the Mitumba males attacked the helpless old girl and beat her up badly. She died of an internal haemorrhage a few days later.

Frodo fled because he was outnumbered. It wasn't honourable but it was sensible. Little Tarzan escaped too, but he had lost his mother. From then on, his mind was shaped both by the nightmare he had witnessed and by having to grow up on his own. Titan, his elder brother, kept him company and Frodo occasionally let him travel with him, but otherwise Tarzan had to fend for himself. This he has done and, as a result, he has become hardened.

I have digressed from Fanni exercising her choice. Returning to her set of possible suitors, from about 2006 she changed her allegiances from Sheldon to Wilkie and they started building a close relationship. They had known each other for a long time, 25 years in fact, and Wilkie began to court Fanni assiduously. Then, in 2007, Fanni gave birth to Fadhila. Now, Wilkie is also the father of Faustino, so that means that Fadhila and Faustino are half siblings. However, since Faustino and Fanni are brother and sister it also means that Faustino is Fadhila's uncle. Relationships wouldn't have been so multifarious had Fifi or Fanni followed the usual gene-dispersing custom of emigrating at puberty.

In that June in 2011, it was a lesson in courage to watch plucky little Fadhila. She was nearly four, but we found her to be ever so busy, looking for food and playing with baby brother Fifty who was born when Fadhila was only two. She had been forced to grow up quickly but was coping without complaint.

Fanni reproduces regularly, with short inter-birth intervals that can affect child development. Consider Familia, who was only three years old when Fadhila was born. It meant that Fanni wasn't able to give as much attention to Familia as before. Familia had to reconcile herself with that and this probably toughened her earlier in life than normal. But we could see that she missed the pampering that an infant usually receives. This is quite reminiscent of the phase that Fudge, Familia's elder brother, experienced. The difference is that Fudge went through a phase of depression whereas Familia just got on with life. Overall, though, when you look at the personalities of Fudge and Familia, you can't help but think that they are rather serious introverts. Both come across as somewhat shy and preoccupied with their own condition.

. Familia also shares personality traits with Gremlin's daughter Gaia when Gaia was Familia's age – serious, quiet and unfussy. Maybe it's to do with their similar upbringings: both their mothers were preoccupied with babies, and the two girls often helped out with baby care – Gaia with the twins and Familia with little sister Fadhila.

I was thinking about the characters of Fanni and her family as we watched the family on the move that peaceful June day. Fanni was in the lead with Fifty on her back, enjoying the passing scenery. Fadhila followed yet managed to be busy and Familia leisurely brought up the rear. I couldn't help but think that,

although quite successful, Fanni still comes across as an enigmatic mother. Indeed, there were occasions when apparent inconsistencies in Fanni's behaviour emerged.

Consider the following incidents which occurred within the space of only 15 minutes. Little Fadhila had found a tasty vine and settled down in anticipation of the pleasure of eating it. Fanni saw this, came over, took the vine from Fadhila and ate it herself. (In fact, we have seen Fanni take away food from both Fadhila and Familia on several occasions and eat it herself.) Anyway, a few minutes later the family was on the move and came across Kakombe stream. It's a shallow stream, but Fadhila was apprehensive about fording it. Fanni waited as Fifty shifted further up her back and Fadhila climbed up behind Fifty. Thus the threesome crossed the stream. Incidents like this also indicate that, despite appearances, Fadhila was still a big baby. In fact, every now and then, Fanni let her suckle, much to her obvious pleasure.

There was another example of Fanni's puzzling behaviour towards her kids. This occurred when the family was resting and an exhausted Fifty was fast asleep in Fanni's lap. For no obvious reason, Fanni got up and moved on, with a bewildered, bleary-eyed Fifty clutching his mother. I am willing to bet that neither Fifi nor Gremlin would have interrupted Fifty's sleep for no apparent reason. At times Fanni can be quite hard on her kids.

Nevertheless, Fanni seems to have grown wiser with age. Only Gremlin, Sandi and Sparrow, among females, are older. She does tend to rest more, settling down to daydream in her inimitable manner for large chunks of time after the family has fed. No longer in the shadow of her dominant mother, she is emerging as a secure personality, confident about the course of her life and looking back with satisfaction on her five children growing up.

It was an evening when we were with Frodo and a small group of males walked in, that we first glimpsed the adult Fudge. Fiona remembers noticing his pointed ears, reminding her of Mr Spock from Star Trek. He had an aura of confidence; after all, he was with the big boys, the elite. A few days later, when we met up with him alone, the swagger had gone. He was nervous and on edge, looking for other Kasekelians.

We can't be sure how long it took Fudge to become fully functional in society after his depression following the birth of Fundi. During that trip we made in 2011, he appeared, on the face of it, well adjusted, and the urge to climb up the male hierarchy seemed to have kicked some life into him. Yet there were times when we still found him brooding, sitting apart from the others. It seems odds on that Fudge will turn out to be quite different from the other F dynasty males.

Our search for Fundi that June was fruitless. It was only during our follow-up visit in September, at the height of the dry season, that he chose to show himself to us. I remember that he still had a light, boyish face and, unlike Fudge, appeared to be at ease with his young age. It would probably be a few years before he set his sights on climbing the male hierarchy.

A little get together. Fanni with her infant son Fifty and adolescent son Fundi is taking it easy at Hilltop, waiting for other Kasekelians to finish feeding and then to move on with them to Kakombe valley below.

Fanni and Fifty on a rock in Kahama valley. Fanni rests her head on a branch while Fadhila plays in a puddle on the floor of the valley. Kahama was once a separate community's home when a breakaway group of Kasekelians settled there. In 1974 a war ensued between the two communities and, by 1978, Kahama had been annexed by the Kasekelians.

Former leader, Goblin. When Goblin was a young male, he was determined to work his way up the male hierarchy. His methods were crude and he took a lot of beating from some of the high-ranking males. But Goblin never wavered and fortunately he had a patron in the then leader, Figan, who tried to shield him from retaliation by the other males. Ironically, it was Figan whom Goblin eventually displaced to become a ruthless leader who brooked no opposition.

Tanga. When Goblin was the leader, he jealously guarded any female who appeared sexually attractive, rushing to intimidate any male who dared to take an interest in an alluring female. During the last year of his reign, he kept a close eye on Tatti and mated with her repeatedly. The outcome was Tanga, who bears a remarkable likeness to her father.

Then: Fanni often struck a pose in which she seemed lost in thought. This pose seems unique to her; I have never seen any other Kasekelian like this. She sleeps like this after her baby has suckled and it's time to take a break.

Now: even today, Fanni still puts her hand on her
forehead when lying down, as if some small detail
is weighing on her mind.

Seven-year-old Familia, Fanni's first daughter. Familia
came after Fudge and Fundi. Fadhila was born next,
when Familia was barely three. Fanni immediately
switched her love and care to Fadhila, leaving Familia
to cope as best she could. Somehow she managed,
but she misplaced her extrovert personality,
withdrawing into an inner world.

Three-year-old Fadhila, Fanni's second daughter. The attention Fadhila received in her first two years, she lost when Fifty was born. Fadhila went from a high to a low – but not too low, since Familia, bearing no grudge, gave her moral support. As a result, Fadhila began to develop a personality marked by resourcefulness, even though, deprived of milk, she is noticeably small.

Kris with Fanni and her son Fundi. Kris was a popular male with the females. On this occasion, he had sought out Fanni's company. Fanni had greeted him with respect and the two stayed together for a while.

Nine-month-old Fifty with mother Fanni. Fanni had found a tasty titbit to eat, whereupon Fifty's curiosity was aroused. First, he wanted to know what it was and then he wanted a bite. Fanni let him – over time I got the impression that Fanni would not refuse Fifty anything. Incidentally, Fifty looks remarkably like Fanni when she was Fifty's age.

Sandi (above) and Apollo (right). 38-year-old Sandi is the eldest surviving child of Sparrow, the matriarch of the S Dynasty. In her youth Sandi was very close to her mother. She was also quite nervous around big groups, relaxing a little if Sparrow or Apollo was around. She and Apollo thus began a friendship that grew and grew. In due course, Apollo courted and mated with Sandi and, as a result, Sampson, Sandi's second child, was born. Apollo also sired Sandi's fourth child, Siri.

Then: seven-year-old Sampson. When Sampson was an infant, Sandi was very nervous about letting him mix with the other Kasekelians. She would sit apart, preferably in a tree if one was handy, ready to grab Sampson at a hint of trouble. Gradually she relented, much to his delight, and very often he was found in the thick of social melees.

Now: 17-year-old Sampson is beginning to assert himself. He dominates all the females and is working his way up the male hierarchy. He roams independently of Sandi and clearly regards himself as a pukka male. Nevertheless, he is still very close to Sandi and, whenever they chance to meet, they spend quality time together.

Apollo (above) and Siri (right). Apollo is easily recognised by his bright and colourful eyes, which his children Siri and Sampson have inherited from him.

Then: three-year-old Tarzan taking a ride on his large-sized mother, Tatti. Tarzan's father is Frodo, also renowned for his size. When Tarzan was a little older, Frodo persuaded Tatti to go on a consortship with him near the border with Mitumba Community. There, Tatti died from a surprise attack by the Mitumban males. Frodo and Tarzan escaped and, ever since, Tarzan has been on his own.

Now: 13-year-old Tarzan. Not adult yet, slightly-built Tarzan should grow to be big, thanks to his parents who were both huge. Today, Tarzan wanders on his own and stays at a respectful distance from the big males, watching them closely. I get the impression that he is taking his time, getting ready to take his chance when the time comes.

Fadhila and younger brother Fifty. The age difference between the two is about two years and eight months and, in the picture on the left, this difference shows in their relative sizes. In the picture on the right, two years later, Fadhila and Fifty are hardly distinguishable by size. Fadhila would normally have suckled till the age of five, but Fanni reduced Fadhila's suckling drastically when Fifty was born.

Full brother and sister, Familia (left) and Fudge (right).
Fanni gave birth to Fundi when Fudge was only three and
she repeated this pattern by giving birth to Fadhila when
Familia was also only three. As Fanni concentrated on
nurturing Fadhila, Familia just got on with life. But when
Fanni had given her full attention to Fundi, Fudge had
descended into a phase of depression.

Chapter 5: **The New Order**

The year 2004 ended very wet. The October rains had arrived in full force and continued through December. Gombe's trails became craters full of rainwater. The Kasekelians disliked the wetness but had to get on with their lives, and 2005 began with Kris firmly entrenched as leader. For a couple of years he had an easy time of it. There were no challenges to his authority, though Apollo and Gimble both seemed a little peeved not to be leaders themselves. But they did reluctantly adjust. Sheldon, like the old guard – Freud, Frodo and Wilkie – had decisively opted for a more relaxing lifestyle, away from the hurly burly of politics. There was a calm atmosphere until, in early 2007, a young male started testing Kris.

The common wisdom had been that one day Faustino would plot a path to the leadership and take it back to the F dynasty. To understand what did happen, it's worth looking at events in Faustino's childhood.

When Faustino was only three, Fifi gave birth to Ferdinand. Faustino still needed his mother's care but Fifi was preoccupied with the new baby. Faustino reacted by becoming increasingly introverted. His playfulness receded and he acquired a serious demeanour. At one point he developed a fungus infection. He recovered but the infection may have weakened him a little. Next, though, came a much more serious condition – a disease that affected his motor nerves. He couldn't coordinate his movements; when he attempted to walk, he would stumble and fall. Walking in a straight line became an impossible task, life an impossible situation. In time, though, he recovered and began to function normally.

Ferdinand, meanwhile, blossomed. He attached himself to elder brother Freud and tried to follow him everywhere. He watched Freud and the other males and stored his observations in the recesses of his brain. Fifi, Freud, Frodo and Faustino indulged him, boosting his confidence. In fact, he developed a close relationship with Faustino, who incidentally bore no grudge, and the brothers forged an understanding of each other's moods and intentions. In 2007, Ferdinand was healthy, intelligent and loved. He was also ambitious and was still only 15.

Slowly but surely, Ferdinand started working on Kris. Actually, he had thought out his strategy in a detached manner. The first stage of the plan was to unsettle Kris, making sure that Faustino was around when he worked on him. Thus began Ferdinand's systematic harassment of the leader.

Ferdinand began to display in Kris's presence – an affront to Kris's status as leader – making sure Faustino joined in. Together, the duo put on electrifying exhibitions of power. It was a calculated way of breaking Kris's nerve. And Kris didn't dare counter-display against these two young but powerful brothers, which gave Ferdinand the signal to ratchet up the pressure.

So Ferdinand started ambushing Kris. His surprise attacks left Kris bewildered. At first, Faustino was around to back up Ferdinand just in case Kris put up a fight. But then Ferdinand preyed on Kris even when Faustino wasn't on hand, confident that Kris wouldn't fight back, and so raised the scale of his harassment.

One fine morning there was a large group of Kasekelians gathered together, including Ferdinand, Faustino and Kris. The atmosphere was relaxed – most were grooming and others were just resting. After a while, Ferdinand detached himself from the group and started rocking to and fro so as to build himself up for a major display. Having worked himself up, he got up and charged right through the group, whereupon all the females and young cleared out of his way. Ferdinand made for Kris and bit his foot hard. Kris cried out and screamed. Even when Ferdinand had quietened down, Kris continued to scream. His nerves had been shattered.

The feedback Ferdinand got from his attack was that he could pick on Kris at opportune moments and that Kris wouldn't retaliate. He also learnt something about violence as a weapon of terror.

Normally, when a Kasekelian male displays and charges he doesn't intend to hurt anyone. The display merely gives out information: 'Look at my strength and power and be very impressed.' But Ferdinand had found out that attacking with the intention of hurting made the Kasekelians very wary of him. They were frightened. It broke an unwritten convention among Kasekelians, but it served Ferdinand's purpose. So Ferdinand put this form of terrorism into practice by ambushing and hurting Kris whenever the opportunity arose. It was no-holds-barred from then on. The harassment was relentless.

Kris realised that he had no options. Ferdinand was too cunning and had the support of Faustino. So Kris surrendered and Ferdinand became the undisputed leader of Kasekela Community in March 2008. The leadership was back with the F dynasty. Ferdinand was only 16.

Even though Kris had surrendered, Ferdinand wouldn't leave him alone. Ferdinand wanted to do a pukka job – he wanted to remove Kris from the group forever. This ruthless streak may come as a surprise, but then Ferdinand was after absolute power. He continued with his persecution of Kris, even though Kris usually managed to avoid him. But one day, about two years after Ferdinand had become the leader, a group of Kasekelians was on the move. In the group was Kris, noticeable by severe injuries on his body. Ferdinand had beaten him up badly and it was the last time anyone saw Kris.

Once Kris had gone, Ferdinand's ruthless streak vanished. He relaxed. His whole bearing acquired self-assurance and his body language exuded confidence. Gradually, the Community caught the vibes and a period of calm ensued. Babies were born, there was an influx of female immigrants, and no one died.

That June 2011, Fiona and I set out to sit with Ferdinand. We walked past the bubbling Kakombe stream and then climbed up Kakombe valley, occasionally slipping at the steep sections and getting tangled in vines. We bumped into Frodo and Tom and stayed with them. Then in the evening, walking along a trail, there came an entourage of males. In the middle, looking every inch a king, was Ferdinand. He took my breath away. The skinny lad of a decade ago had filled out. His face was darker, his eyes spoke experience. He looked sure of himself and he exuded dignity. There was a gravitas about him.

Ferdinand wasn't the biggest Kasekelian. Titan was, and already he was at number three in the rankings, after Faustino at number two. Thinking about the rankings as we were climbing in search of Kasekelians one morning, it seemed that Titan could soon prove to be a serious challenger to Ferdinand.

It was at Bald Soko, on the yellow grassy plain, that we came across a small group of Kasekelians. 17-year-old Titan was in the group as was his younger brother, Tarzan. I at once could see that Titan, son of Frodo and Tatti, had inherited the bulk and strength of his parents.

We sat down near the Kasekelians, who ignored us, and watched them groom. I noticed one difference between Titan at 17 and the younger Titan. Now he seemed to conserve energy. Back then, in 2001 to 2003, he was a live grenade of energy. Even his sister Tanga, five years older than him, would tire of playing with him. Then Titan would think of games to play by himself, crazy games such as covering himself with dry leaves over and over again.

Poor Tatti had had a tough time weaning Titan off milk. Indeed, his pleas and tantrums for milk were terrifying. But somehow Tatti succeeded. Then she had baby Tarzan when Titan was six years old and so pretty soon she had another headache to deal with. Titan wanted to play with Tarzan on his terms, and the play would get so rough that either Tatti or Tanga would have to rescue Tarzan. Fortunately for harassed Tatti, Titan often got distracted by the lure of the big males. As I recall, he was totally fearless and would approach them unfazed, occasionally getting caught up in a fracas.

As for the older Titan versus Ferdinand, my guess was that, one-on-one, Titan was stronger than his uncle (Frodo, elder brother of Ferdinand, is Titan's dad) and would win a trial of strength. What was telling, however, was Titan's lack of self-belief when compared to Ferdinand's enormous confidence. When it came to the mental game – and a tussle for leadership is, in the long run, a mental battle – Ferdinand was still ahead.

In addition, Titan didn't appear to have friends to back him up – apart from Faustino, who would have been expected to support his brother Ferdinand in any leadership challenge. Titan seemed to have inherited Frodo's social ineptitude and didn't spend enough time building alliances. But then, during our later trips, we noticed that Titan had started to work on gaining support. And it is worth taking into account that, in kid brother Tarzan, Titan could have a strong ally in the future.

We watched the full brothers, 11-year-old Tarzan and Titan, groom each other. Would they be allies in the future and take Ferdinand on? I wasn't sure. Tarzan appeared to have a mind of his own and a chip on his shoulder. He might prefer to go for the leadership on his own when the time came. To me, he appeared to be the type of guy who would want to climb to the summit of the male hierarchy alone, come what may.

Tarzan certainly had attitude. I recall one clear incident when Tarzan snubbed Ferdinand. It was on an afternoon in early July in a shady elevation overlooking the lake. Here, by chance, Tarzan and Ferdinand had come together. Ferdinand presented his back to Tarzan, a request for grooming. Tarzan blatantly ignored it and walked away. Ferdinand seemed to let it go.

But a few days later Tarzan got a drubbing from Ferdinand. It was morning and he was sitting apart from the trio of Ferdinand, Apollo and 23-year-old Nasa, who was trying her best to mate with Ferdinand. He finally obliged and then all three started grooming. It was during this session that they heard a rustling sound in the thicket above them. In a flash, Nasa and Ferdinand dashed into the thicket, followed by a slow-footed Apollo. Nasa grabbed a four-year-old baboon which she and Ferdinand pulled in two. Amid great excitement, Apollo and Tarzan noisily begged for a share of the meat. Maybe Tarzan pushed his luck, something not beyond his character, or maybe Ferdinand recalled the snub of a few days earlier. In any case, Ferdinand reprimanded him so severely that with loud cries of anguish Tarzan retired to the fringes, moaning to himself. Much later, he obsequiously approached Ferdinand who ignored him completely. It seemed as if Tarzan wanted to apologise but Ferdinand made him sweat for a while.

I digress. Returning to the topic of the struggle to the top, it seems that Titan is the obvious challenger to Ferdinand. Faustino is unlikely to take on his brother for the number one spot and those who appear to be rising through the ranks, Sampson and Fudge, seem to have some way to go before they can be realistically vying for the leadership.

Sampson has such a distinctive face that we were quite curious to find out if I could recognise him after a gap of ten years. One mid-June morning in 2011, after a rough climb up a slope through the tangles of undergrowth, we came across him sitting on a trail looking as only Sampson could. It was clear that he was just a kid compared to Ferdinand, even though he was already 15 years old. The trouble with Sampson was twofold: he had a slender build and he had yet to reveal any sign of the ruthless streak that Ferdinand himself had at that age. Despite having powerfully built, 28-year-old Sheldon as an uncle, the two had never formed a political alliance. The upshot was that Sampson was no match for Ferdinand on his own, and they both knew it. He wisely kept out of Ferdinand's way. Since Fudge was also in awe of Ferdinand, that left Titan as the only one with enough physical strength to have a realistic chance of overthrowing Ferdinand – up to that point, anyway.

Given that Ferdinand was the leader, Faustino was number two and Titan number three – Frodo should have been happy. After all, Frodo was the elder brother of the first two and the father of the third. Actually, Frodo had done quite well since he was also the father of the mild-mannered Zeus and stockily built Sinbad. Frodo also had a stake in the G dynasty, having mated with Gremlin and thereby sired the twins Golden and Glitter. Actually, Gremlin, with Gaia's help, had done well raising the twins. They were 13 years old in that June of 2011 and on the threshold of being mothers themselves. As chance would have it, Fiona and I saw them on the very first day of our visit to Kasekela that year.

Kasekelians on the beach. In the southern part of the Community, close to the shore of Lake Tanganyika, there are two groups of mango trees about a kilometre apart. Having checked out the first group of trees at a place called Kahama, Ferdinand led the way, hugging the beach, to the second group at Nyasanga.

Brothers and allies. Together, Ferdinand (right) and Faustino (above) have absolute power, and the confidence that imparts shows in their demeanour. Funny how sometimes history repeats itself. Just as Faustino is an able second in command and rallies to support the leader, so once upon a time did Faben, brother and ally of Figan. On the other hand, Freud and Frodo were brothers and competitors.

Ferdinand. At 20, he exudes confidence. He is sure
of himself and his actions are well thought out
and measured. Ferdinand is really a faster version
of Freud in his prime in that he first observes, then
thinks, and then acts – seemingly leisurely but
actually quite quickly.

Titan. The 18-year-old Titan today conserves energy, which is quite unlike the Titan of ten years ago, who seemed in perpetual motion. He also spends a lot of time on his own, walking long distances at a steady pace. Titan has great strength, but little tact. He is ambitious but unpopular, commanding respect but not affection.

Ferdinand, Pax and Apollo (from right to left). While
the lowest-ranking male, Pax, stays discreetly in
the background, middle-ranking Apollo looks
admiringly at top-ranking Ferdinand. And there
you have it – a leader with great self-assurance, a
low-ranking male who ingratiates himself to the
top command, and the lowest-ranking male who
knows his place in any social set-up.

Tarzan. Although only 13, he often acts like an adult. A thinker too, he appears to be the type of guy who will do things his way. For the moment he is in no-man's-land – the adult males don't take him seriously and he has no firm friends in his peer group. I like to think of him as a dark horse.

Sampson. When Sampson was 15 years old, he didn't
make much of an impression physically. He was just a
slender kid without a ruthless streak. Then a year passed,
he became bulkier, more confident and more assertive.
Another year passed and he had arrived as a male,
acknowledged as such by all the females – though, for
the moment, he is ranked very low in the male hierarchy.

Fudge. Unlike Sampson, he was quick off the mark in climbing up the male hierarchy and now ranks at number five. That he is a nephew of Ferdinand and Faustino, the top-ranking duo, obviously helps.

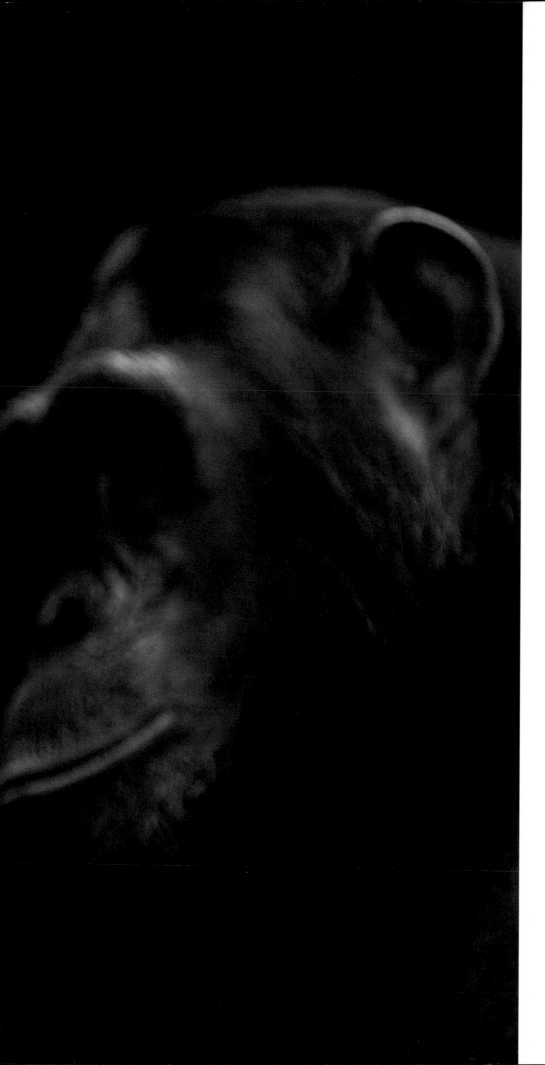

Golden grooming Frodo. Frodo also had a stake in the G Dynasty, being the father of the twins, Golden and Glitter. Since he was also the father of Zeus, Sinbad, Samwise, Titan and Tarzan, you could say that his genes have been spread wide. In terms of evolutionary success, Frodo has done extremely well.

Chapter 6: **Strange Happenings in the G Dynasty**

Fiona and I left the boat, stowed our luggage in the rest house overlooking the lake and began the hike up the steep hill behind the house. We hadn't gone far before we got our first glimpse of the twins. We saw them grooming each other but couldn't see their faces. As we drew closer, they turned to look at us. In place of the two happy-go-lucky kids that I remembered from ten years before, we saw two refined adults. It was difficult to associate their faces with those of the two jovial kids. We sat with them for about half an hour and then left them when they moved on to look for food.

Later we learnt that the twins were pregnant. Normally, the transition from pregnancy to motherhood would have been a smooth affair, but fate had other ideas and, over the next eight months, a few bizarre incidents took place. To understand what happened we need to look at the experiences of the twins' elder sister, Gaia.

Gaia was born on Valentine's Day, 1993. Two days later, Gremlin was feeding in a tree, cradling Gaia with one hand against her chest. Five-year-old Galahad, Gaia's elder brother, was feeding nearby. Presently, Fifi arrived with infant Ferdinand and was followed by the rest of her offspring – four-year-old Faustino, eight-year-old Flossi and twelve-year-old Fanni with her infant son Fax. Soon they were joined by Gigi, another high-ranking female.

Led by Gigi, they climbed into Gremlin's tree. Fifi seemed mesmerised by baby Gaia, staring at her hard. Gremlin was nervous and submissive but at the same time tried to shade Gaia away from Fifi's hostile eyes. After a brief pause, Fifi, Fanni and Gigi began to close in on Gremlin.

The trio followed Gremlin further up the tree and then attacked her with kicks, slaps and punches. Gremlin, crouching over a terrified Gaia, cried and screamed as she tried to fend off the blows, but she was trapped. Just then, Tatti arrived, accompanied by three other Kasekelians.

The attacks stopped. A stalemate followed and after 15 minutes the aggressors left. Tatti stayed a while and then left as daylight faded. Gremlin saw her leave and, together with Galahad, went hurriedly in the opposite direction as darkness closed around the small G family.

Gaia had grown up in the shadow of her precocious brother, Galahad. When she was five and Galahad ten, Gremlin gave birth to the twins Golden and Glitter. At first, a nervous Gremlin tried to keep away from the rest of the Kasekelians. But two days after the birth, when Gremlin and her family were resting on the ground, Frodo arrived unexpectedly. Frodo was the leader then and also in an unpredictable mood. Fearful, Gremlin froze. Frodo spotted the twins at once and was immediately fascinated. A tender expression appeared on his face and Gremlin relaxed. Perhaps this was to be expected – he was their father after all. Just then, Fanni arrived with 18-month-old Fudge. She spotted the twins right away and promptly sat down close to Gremlin, staring hard at the twins. A visibly agitated Gremlin sought Frodo's protection as Fanni kept following, her eyes fixed on the twins. Her intentions did not seem benign. Fortunately, Gremlin managed to stay with Frodo all the time until Fanni left them at mid-morning.

Events took a dramatic turn in the afternoon. Gremlin was resting on the ground when she saw Fifi, Ferdinand, Faustino, Fanni and Fudge approaching. Gremlin quickly sat up, holding the twins close to her chest. Ferdinand and Faustino tried to get a view of the twins, but Galahad and Gaia stood between them, and Gremlin looked threatening. But when Fifi and Fanni got closer, Gremlin turned and walked away with her family. As Fifi and Fanni followed, she broke into a run but was pursued determinedly. Fifi and Fanni caught up with Gremlin and, after a tense stand-off, attacked her. Gremlin retaliated whereupon Fanni repeatedly pounded Gremlin on the head as Gremlin, hunched over the twins, punched back. Fifi joined in and the three females grappled, screaming loudly. Galahad and Gaia watched horrified.

Gremlin broke away and ran, supporting the twins with one hand and screaming loudly. Fifi and Fanni followed, trying to grab the hair on Gremlin's back. Gremlin rushed up a tree but then ran out of space to run into. Trying to dislodge her, Fifi shook the branch Gremlin was sitting on, but that didn't work. Fifi herself was heavily pregnant and was finding it hard to keep her balance. There then began a tense stand-off which lasted for about an hour. Finally, Fifi and Fanni gave up and left. Gremlin, immensely relieved, descended and walked in the opposite direction with Gaia and Galahad, who had helplessly watched the entire encounter. It must have been difficult for the two of them to comprehend what had happened.

There were no further aggressive incidents after that and, for the next couple of years, Gremlin somehow managed to cope with bringing up the twins. Meanwhile Galahad was growing up fast, preoccupied with being in the company of the big boys. It seemed likely that in the near future he would be speedily climbing the male hierarchy. Instead Galahad ran out of time, succumbing to a fatal respiratory infection at the age of 12.

Somehow Gremlin coped with both the loss of her son and caring for the twins. She would balance the twins on her body as she climbed trees, suckle them while Gaia demanded attention, and try to keep out of the way of other Kasekelians. Surprisingly, but fortunately for Gremlin, Fifi and Fanni had resumed their friendship with her and lost interest in taking her twins away.

The pressure on Gremlin eased when Gaia became more attentive to the twins. She became very useful when her mother tried to wean the twins, since as soon as Gremlin succeeded in denying one, the other would resume her demand for milk, and Gaia distracted the twins by keeping them occupied. Finally the twins were weaned and it seemed as if a burden had been lifted off Gremlin's shoulders. On the other hand, Gaia's childhood had slipped by. She had not interacted much with other Kasekelians of her age. She was firmly in the process of identifying herself as Gremlin's daughter, loyal and obedient, her own personality suppressed.

At about the age of 11, Gaia began to lead an existence independent of Gremlin, although mother and daughter did meet up often and spend time together. Gaia was also in the vicinity when Gremlin gave birth to Gimli in January 2004. Soon after the birth, Gremlin, with her five-year-old twins in tow, came across the then leader, Sheldon, and a few other Kasekelians: her brother Gimble, Gaia, and also Fifi and Fanni. Fifi and Fanni immediately noticed Gimli and took more than a curious interest in the newborn. Gremlin picked up on this quickly and immediately sought the protection of Sheldon and Gimble. Fifi

and Fanni continued to stare hard at Gimli. Their intentions seemed hostile. Gaia sensed this too and slipped next to Gremlin, prepared for an onslaught. But the presence of the males seemed to restrain Fifi and Fanni. Gremlin managed to stay with the males and, realising this, Fifi and Fanni gave up their intimidation.

Fifi hadn't been seen for a year and a half when Gaia, 13, gave birth to Godot. I suppose Gaia was streetwise to the possible danger posed by Fanni to her newborn, and I think she was quite capable of looking after herself and Godot should Fanni turn up and strike. But, as fate would have it, the threat to Gaia's baby came from an unexpected quarter.

A couple of days after Godot's birth, Gaia and Gremlin, with three-year-old Gimli, were sitting together when Fanni, with her children, chanced upon them. Gremlin and Gaia watched apprehensively as Fanni approached them. Then, although Fanni showed no signs of outward aggression, Gremlin reached out and took Godot away from Gaia. Always respectful and trustful of her mother, Gaia let her. The encounter with Fanni fizzled out, but what happened subsequently will always remain an unsolved puzzle.

What transpired was this: Gremlin held on to Godot and Gaia made no attempt to get him back. She was an obedient daughter and probably trusted Gremlin to know what was best for Godot. But deep inside, she must have yearned to get her baby back, to hold and nurture him. Thus it came to pass that Gremlin started looking after both Godot and Gimli. However, Gremlin faced an awkward problem in bringing up both. Gimli, with his larger appetite, drank most of Gremlin's milk. As a consequence, Godot grew weaker. He eventually became listless and died at five months of age in Gremlin's lap, malnourished and tiny in size – much to Gremlin's surprise.

Now it may be advanced, given Fanni's history of hostility to Gremlin's newborn babies, that Gremlin acted reasonably, believing that Godot was safer with her than with Gaia. But then another incident occurred that cast doubt on Gremlin's sagacity. Nearly two years after Godot's birth, Gaia gave birth to a set of twins. This was unusual in itself, but what was more unusual was that Gremlin took one twin away from Gaia and, once again, Gaia didn't protest. She may have felt a wrench, but again she wouldn't take on her mother.

Gremlin tried to look after the snatched baby but she wasn't lactating. The baby died in her arms within a week of its birth, much to her surprise and dismay. So Gremlin took the other twin from Gaia and it died the same death. Perhaps Gremlin was a well-meaning grandmother, trying to do good but not thinking about the consequences. Sadly, Gaia had now lost three babies. Her life as a mother had got off to a tragic start.

But Gaia became pregnant again and gave birth in June 2009 to a male, Google. She was now wise to her mother's penchant for newborn babies and skilfully managed to avoid her in the early days of Google's life. Then, two and a half months later, Gaia got a break: Gremlin herself gave birth to a baby boy, Gizmo. As a result, Gremlin was fully occupied looking after tiny Gizmo, allowing

Gaia to range more freely. However, whenever she came into contact with her mother she was watchful and possessive. She need not have worried, though, since Gremlin made no attempt to snatch her grandson – accepting, finally, the natural way of things.

It's puzzling that Gremlin had on three occasions taken charge of tiny babies. What was she thinking? A clue to her mind came in July 2011, when an incident occurred that changed the life of Glitter, one of the twins.

When the twins reached the age of 12 there had arisen the possibility that one or both of them would emigrate to either the Mitumba Community to the north or the Kalande Community to the south. Furthermore, since they spent a lot of time together, it seemed likely that if they did emigrate, then they would do it together. But as it turned out neither Glitter nor Golden made any attempt to leave Kasekela. In fact, Glitter gave birth to a baby girl on 10 July, 2011. Baby G was born healthy and Glitter could look forward to bringing her up. But she had reckoned without Gremlin.

And a few days after the birth, Gremlin struck. She took Baby G away from Glitter. Unlike Gaia, Glitter tried to get her baby back. But Gremlin was firm in her decision and Glitter didn't press her case – for a good reason as the following incident illustrates. The G family were together and Gaia reached out to take something that Gremlin was holding. Gremlin reacted unexpectedly. Bristling, she attacked Gaia and the two fell on the ground, grappling. Gaia managed to wriggle free and apologise to Gremlin who cooled down. Clearly, Gremlin is a formidable female of great strength and her daughters are in awe of her. They know that she will get her way, by force if she chooses.

Then events took a strange turn. At the time that Gremlin snatched Glitter's baby, she was accompanied by seven-year-old Gimli and two-year-old Gizmo, who was still suckling. What happened next was that two or three weeks after Gremlin had taken Glitter's baby, Glitter took Gizmo. When you think about it, there was a logic to it. If Glitter couldn't have her baby back then Gizmo would do. Gremlin seemed happy enough with the arrangement; Gizmo was mobile and could run around on his own, and he would be okay as long as Glitter suckled and protected him. As for Gremlin, she now had an infant to look after and could indulge in her adoration of babies. Gizmo, though, had other ideas.

Whereas it's fine for your elder sister to look after you and even suckle you, she is not a substitute for Mummy. After a few days, Gizmo went back to Gremlin. This was fine with Gremlin, but there was a consequence for Gizmo. It should be said that there is a strong bond between Glitter and Gizmo. Over the course of two years we often saw Glitter carrying him, grooming him and playing with him. In fact, Gizmo would excitedly run to Glitter whenever she turned up to visit Gremlin. By way of comparison, Gizmo has never shown the same level of affection for either of his other two sisters, Golden and Gaia.

Whenever we encountered Gremlin with Baby G, we noticed that Baby G was alert and lively. She would wriggle to get a good look at us and keep us in view.

For her part, Gremlin was very attentive to Baby G and clearly adored her. In fact, it turned out that Gremlin had more time for Baby G than Gizmo. Consequently, Gizmo felt neglected and became withdrawn. Whereas previously he had been at the centre of Gremlin's world, he was now at the periphery. He would occasionally perk up when either Gimli or Glitter played with him, but the flush of delight didn't linger for long once play ended. Then something brilliant happened.

Five weeks after Glitter had given birth, Golden gave birth – which, in hindsight, was well timed. Gremlin was too busy with baby G and Gizmo to pay any more attention than normal to the new arrival. Both Baby G and Gizmo were suckling and that meant that Gremlin needed to spend a lot of time gathering food to eat and to produce the milk demanded by the young ones.

In view of what happened next, it's worth reiterating that Gremlin is an experienced mother with intimate touches. In fact, once Gremlin, Gimli and Gizmo had come across Sandi with four-year-old son Siri feeding in an mbula fruit tree. For a while all individuals were settled, feeding, playing or resting. There was tranquillity in the dim forest. Then Gremlin decided to move on, gathering up Gizmo. However, glancing up, she saw that Gimli was still playing with Siri in the tree. So she sat down and patiently waited for Gimli to finish playing. While they waited, Gizmo got bored and restless. Quick to notice this, Gremlin stuck her hand out and rolled Gizmo on the ground, amusing him greatly. It was only when Gimli descended of his own accord that the trio moved on.

Gimli is a precocious lad. He is also intrepid. He often led the foursome – himself, Gremlin, Gizmo, Baby G – when it was on the move, darting here and there to investigate anything that caught his eye. Once he spotted a large monitor lizard and, without hesitation, chased it. The frightened lizard took off at great speed, pursued by a gleeful Gimli. The lizard was faster and escaped as Gimli slowed down to watch it go. A few days later, while traversing the cool Kakombe valley, the trio came across a troop of baboons loitering in their path. While the others sat and watched, Gimli went straight ahead, a palm frond in his hand, and displayed. That didn't impress the baboons. Undeterred, he picked up a stick and went charging into the baboons but was still not able to get a reaction. Then, unexpectedly, a female baboon calmly presented herself to him. Curious, Gimli examined her swelling before losing interest.

During our visit in May 2012, we caught up with Gimli. He was again up to mischief, throwing stones with a very bad aim at male baboons and investigating a snake he had encountered. On our fourth visit, in September and October of 2012, we noticed that Gimli had graduated to chasing fully-grown male baboons. No male baboon took offence and retaliated, aware perhaps of Gremlin's presence. On another occasion he darted into the bush and came out with a mouse in his hand. Watched by a fascinated younger brother, Gimli killed the mouse, carried it on his back and placed it on his thigh when he sat down. Gimli also got excited whenever he spotted an adult male. He would boldly run up to greet him and then imitate the male's walk, swagger and display.

Golden, meanwhile, was having no trouble keeping her baby Glamour from Gremlin. Initially, she was cautious and kept her distance. Then, over the next few days, she came nearer but was careful not to show Glamour's face to Gremlin. Only when the bond between her and Glamour was stronger and Gremlin continued to show no interest in stealing Glamour, did Golden come to within touching distance of Gremlin. After that, a change took place in her routine. Instead of travelling alone or with Glitter, she began travelling with Gremlin, secure in the knowledge that Gremlin had no intention of taking her baby. After all, Gremlin was an excellent mother and grandmother when she wasn't interested in pinching the babies of her daughters. Gremlin also often avoided big gatherings of Kasekelians which suited Golden fine.

Golden settled into being a mother. Whenever we saw her, we could tell that she was gentle and attentive towards her baby. She also played a lot with Glamour, often tickling her, too. Glamour was big at birth and continued to grow well. Her chances of surviving and thriving seemed excellent.

For Baby G, on the other hand, it was touch and go. In mid-January 2012 she looked fine, if small for her age. Then she took a turn for the worse. She kept crying and became progressively weaker, then listless. It became inevitable: at the age of just six months she died in Gremlin's arms on 21 January 2012. Gremlin was distressed. She kept opening Baby G's eyes and checking her breathing. She carried her for a couple of days and then, unusually, Gimli carried her around too. After that, Baby G was discarded. As for Glitter, no one can guess the grief she must have been going through ever since losing her baby to her mother.

Overleaf: Gremlin calling. Gaia, in the background, is calling too. The location is Kakombe valley, which Gremlin treats as her own. When in the valley, Gremlin doesn't usually reveal her location, but in this instance, several males called and she thought it wise to reply, thereby communicating her position.

The twins. At 14, not only do the twins look different,
they also have differing personalities. Golden (right) is
social, trusting and extroverted. Glitter (above) is more
of a loner, a little wary and quite introverted. As for
the relationship between the two, Golden is the more
assertive. Thus you find Glitter grooming her twin sister
a lot but not getting much grooming back in return.

Gaia. Due to bizarre circumstances, Gaia had lost three babies by the age of 16, including a set of twins. The culprit was her mother, Gremlin, who inexplicably snatched Gaia's newborns but failed to keep them alive. Then Gaia gave birth to Google and with him her fortune as a mother seemed to have changed.

Google aged two. He is bold, mischievous and smart. Once Gremlin was apart from the G's and called to Gaia to join her. Google listened attentively but Gaia paid no attention, engrossed in termite-fishing. Gremlin called again and Google made as if to go, but Gaia stayed fishing. After a while, Gremlin called again and this time Google looked at Gaia and at the source of the sound. When he got Gaia's attention, he walked away and stopped watching her. When Gaia got up and made as if to gather him up and return to the termite mound, he moved away. Gaia was in a dilemma. As she moved to catch Google he moved further away. He thus led her further away from the mound and induced her to join Gremlin.

Google at three. Google is especially curious and quick to investigate anything that catches his eye. An interesting fact is that while on a journey and when he is not riding on Gaia's back, Google will often lead and dart here and there. Gaia lets him be, waiting patiently for Google to get bored with whatever he has got absorbed in and come back to her. Then they resume their journey.

Gremlin at 42. Gremlin has given birth to eight kids to date. Her first three died, but the five that followed are doing well. Now Gremlin appears to be slowing down and is partial to comforts. Once, when a largish group of females with kids was resting, Gremlin took the opportunity to make herself even more comfortable by scraping a shallow hole in the ground to lie in; and she managed to make the hole match the contours of her back.

Gizmo at two. He is Gremlin's eighth child and she looks out for him. Once, Gimli wanted to termite-fish at the hole vacated by Gremlin, as did Gizmo. Gremlin intervened and told Gimli to let Gizmo have a go first. Gimli obliged, and a happy Gizmo got to try his luck at termite-fishing.

Mother and son playing. Gaia is very attentive towards her son Google and often plays with him for long stretches at a time. A consequence is that Gaia and Google look a close-knit pair. Their play may be out of necessity, since Google is energetic and low-ranking Gaia usually stays on the fringes of social gatherings, denying Google opportunities to play with other youngsters and thereby expend his energy.

Gremlin with Baby G and Gizmo. Gremlin was an odd sight, carrying and suckling both her son Gizmo and her granddaughter Baby G, whom she'd snatched from Glitter. Gremlin was lactating, but Gizmo drank most of the milk, leaving only a little for Baby G. It showed in the size of Baby G, who was small for her age – just over two months old in this picture. At the same time, Gizmo – just over two years old here – hardly ever strayed far from Gremlin, reluctant to join in play with the other kids if it meant being too far from his mother. Perhaps having to share his mother made him feel insecure.

Gremlin drinking from Kakombe stream, using a leaf as a sponge, with Baby G held in her lap. Gizmo is copying her action without much success. On the right, Gaia, having quenched her thirst, is biding her time until Gremlin finishes drinking and moves on. Normally, Gremlin would have put her mouth to the running water to drink from the stream, but carrying Baby G made that an awkward exercise.

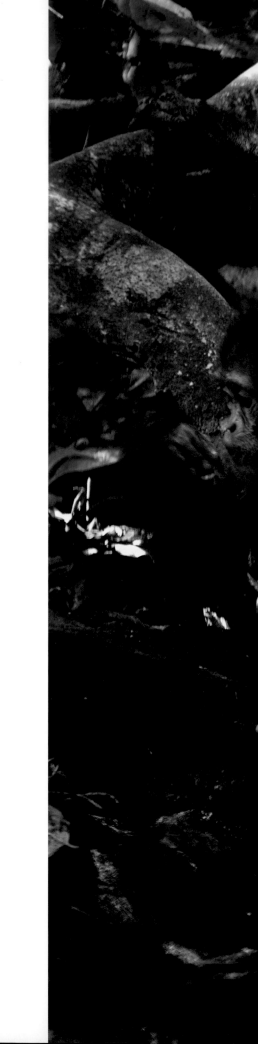

Glitter carrying Gizmo. There is a strong bond between sister Glitter and brother Gizmo. We often saw Glitter carry Gizmo, groom him and play with him. He never showed the same level of interaction with his two other sisters, Golden and Gaia. The bond between Glitter and Gizmo started early on in Gizmo's life but got a boost when Gremlin took Baby G away from Glitter. In turn, Glitter lavished her maternal affection on Gizmo.

Baby G. Although small for her age, Baby G was alert and lively. Upon our arrival, she would wriggle around to get a good look at us and keep us in view. She also had a healthy appetite for Gremlin's milk. But she didn't seem to be growing fast enough. We were unsure about the strength of her immune system, given that Gremlin was at a stage in her lactating cycle where she was producing milk with antibodies suitable for a two-year-old instead of a two-month-old.

Gremlin with Baby G. Ferdinand the leader is in the background. Gremlin was very attentive to Baby G and clearly adored her. In fact, it turned out that she had more time for her granddaughter than her son Gizmo. We found her regularly grooming Baby G, caressing her lovingly and holding her close to her chest when lying down for a rest. No wonder Gizmo felt neglected, often sitting next to Gremlin and feeling sorry for himself.

Gremlin, a veteran of Kasekela. She is also a top-ranking female. She had a rival in Fanni but the two are friends now. Once, Fanni with Fadhila and Fifty joined up with the G's. They fed and rested together. Fifty had a boisterous time, playing with the G kids, including Gimli, until the group broke up and the families went their separate ways. Fanni slipped her hand in Gremlin's who acknowledged the gesture and then Fanni was off. It was goodbye and thank you.

Gremlin entertaining Gizmo. As a mother, Gremlin has intimate touches. Once she had to stop walking when Gimli veered off to explore. She sat with Gizmo, who started to get fidgety. Sensing Gizmo's boredom, Gremlin simply stuck out her hand for him to play with, much to his delight. Gremlin and Gizmo played thus until Gimli returned and the threesome resumed their travels.

Eight-year-old Gimli. He often regarded himself to be the big man in the G family. Once, Fanni was sitting with Fifty when she was approached by Golden with an outstretched hand and Glamour readying herself to play with Fifty. Glitter, with baby Gossamer, was following Golden. Inexplicably, Fanni displayed at the twins, sending them up a tree. Eight-year-old Gimli, who was sitting with Gremlin, saw this from afar and came bounding over. With considerable officiousness, he shepherded the twins safely to Gremlin, not that they needed Gimli's help.

Gimli in a thoughtful mood. A discernible change had quickly come over Gimli. He was really fascinated by the big males and relished being with them, especially Frodo. Gimli could be found sitting admiringly near him or walking behind him, as if irresistibly drawn to him. He also began to display after the males had displayed and gone, making sure no one was looking, and started taking an interest in oestrus females. Once he shook a sapling at Iowyn and sat invitingly with his legs spread apart. Iowyn came over and Gimli obliged.

Eight-year-old Gimli sitting absorbed as the rest of the G family get up to all sorts of things in the background. Earlier, Gimli had been watching elder sister Gaia termite-fishing and Gaia had noticed that Gimli wanted to have a go. She gently gestured by putting her hand on him, as if to say: you have a go now. Then it was rest and social time for the G entourage. Golden, Gaia and Gremlin groomed each other while Gimli, Gizmo and Google played. Then Gimli got bored and sat on his own, contemplating that which only he knows.

Gimli being casual, taking it easy while the others forage. Previously, Gimli had been playing with Google and the game had got quite rough. Gaia vocalised to stop Gimli playing, which he did. After a while, a bored Gimli went to Google to play again, but Gaia stopped him. Gimli looked at Gremlin who assented with Gaia. Gimli at once threw a tantrum. Gizmo got frightened and went to Gaia who was already clutching Google, and she put her arms around both of them. Once his tantrum was over, Gimli apologised to Gremlin by touching her with an outstretched arm.

Golden quenching her thirst. Golden, with Glamour in her lap, found it awkward to drink from Kakombe stream by putting her mouth to the water's surface as is normal. So, she crumpled a leaf and used it like a sponge, soaking it in the stream and then squeezing the moisture into her mouth. She repeated the process until she was satiated.

The G family. Gremlin lies on the ground with Baby G while Golden sleeps in the background. Gizmo is next to Gremlin, and then there is Gaia grooming Gremlin. Google is in a world of his own. Once again, Gimli is sitting apart and Glitter is elsewhere. While the adults take it easy, Gizmo and Google, especially Google, are very active.

Gremlin relaxes with her family. From left to right are Google, Golden with Glamour, Gizmo, Gremlin herself with Baby G and Gaia. Not in the picture is Gimli, sitting a little apart, lost in his own world. Glitter was away – she was sexually receptive and mixing with the males. This situation, in which Kasekelians take time off from foraging, is a testament to the richness of their forest home.

Baby G. Gremlin stopped at Kakombe stream to drink, with Baby G in her lap. Having quenched her thirst, Gremlin waited for her meandering sons. Baby G leant back, but this wasn't to get a better view. It was because she was lethargic. Life was slowly leaving her. She died in Gremlin's arms, just six months old.

Airplane. Golden often played a game with Glamour that we called 'airplane'. Golden would sit and, with a leg, raise Glamour high up, much to Glamour's obvious glee. The fun side of the Golden-Glamour relationship owes a lot to Golden's love of play. In one vigorous session, we saw Glamour roll her on the ground, hug her with delight, tease her and mock-bite her, all with a mischievous glint in her eyes.

Golden and Glamour. No doubt about it, Golden adores Glamour and vice versa. The touching relationship between the two is partly due to Golden's nurturing urge. Her tolerance is high and her patience is vast. She has probably also learnt a lot from her mother.

Chapter 7: **More Bizarre Events in the G Dynasty**

When we returned to Kasekela at the beginning of May 2012, there was much to catch up on. How were Golden and Glamour faring? Was Glitter pregnant? How was Gizmo?

Our concern for Gizmo needs an explanation. He had had a nerve-wracking adventure during our second visit in October 2011. That was when Gremlin was also looking after Baby G and it had been evident that Gizmo was verging on depression. Before Baby G's arrival he had been active and playful. After Baby G's arrival he had become withdrawn, unhappy at being marginalised. It was sad to see him not responding to Google's invitations to play, whiling away his time sitting and brooding. Clearly, he was emotionally dependent on his mother. Then a near-tragedy occurred.

On 11 October 2011, a large group of Kasekelians was moving from Kasekela valley towards Rutanga valley to the north. Five females in the group were at their most attractive, inducing turmoil in the accompanying six males. The others, including Gremlin, Gizmo and Baby G, were keeping to the fringes as the males strutted, charged and displayed to impress the girls. Mid-afternoon found the group scattered and feeding. Gremlin had climbed a tree and let Gizmo off to explore it. Just then, the males broke into a frenzied display. In the bedlam that ensued, Gremlin retreated towards the north while Gizmo panicked and followed the Kasekelians he could see moving south. But they were moving fast and Gizmo got left behind. Meanwhile, Gremlin had realised that Gizmo was nowhere to be seen. She searched frantically, but by this time Gizmo was well and truly out of visual and audible contact. Gremlin continued her search north as a tearful Gizmo wandered south on his own, calling softly for his mother. Then came the night.

Early next morning Fidel, our tracker, came across him – a small, frightened figure. He was moving in the direction of Kakombe valley, which Gremlin visited regularly and which the two-year-old Gizmo was familiar with. He walked the trails his mother often used, but he also crashed out frequently. You can only guess at his mental state. Nevertheless, he somehow made it to Kakombe and stayed there, whimpering softly. It was heart-wrenching. He looked so small and lost in this big forested valley. Meanwhile, Gremlin was located and lured to cross the huge distance separating her from her son. When she was close to Gizmo and about to turn back, Gizmo cried. Gremlin heard and ran fast towards the source of the cry. Next she was hugging her brave little son, who promptly went for a nipple and drank and drank. Gremlin fussed over him and then the two lay down under a shady tree with contented expressions on their faces.

During this third visit of ours we often came across the trio of Gremlin, Gizmo and Gimli, who were ranging in the centre of the Community. A change had come over Gizmo since the passing away of Baby G, and he was more active than we had ever known him to be. He and Gimli would often play whenever Gremlin was resting. Indeed, Gremlin was resting a lot and moving less as, in her old age, physical exertion easily tired her. But even while resting, one of her hands would often be toying with Gizmo. Life was much better for Gizmo now.

Sometimes Gaia and Google would join up with Gremlin for half a day or so, and then Gizmo and Google would have a boisterous time playing while the adults rested or fished for termites. Gimli would join in the fray, then get tired of playing with the young ones and groom the adults or sit and think. When he wanted to move he would carry Gizmo away and groom him, hoping Gremlin would take the cue and follow. Often Gremlin was too tired to move and would continue to rest, whereupon Gizmo would return to Gremlin. Gimli wasn't discouraged when his strategy failed though; he would find something to amuse himself and then try again later.

Golden would also visit Gremlin with Glamour if they were in the vicinity. Although only nine months old, Glamour would play with Gizmo, often giving back as good a thump or bite as she got. She was a brave little thing, being in the rough and tumble without any fear. Watching Glamour play, I was reminded of an earlier occasion involving two different Kasekelian infants interacting. 20-month-old baby boy Nyota wanted to play with 10-month-old baby boy Duke. It wasn't a happy experience for little Duke, who tried to get away from Nyota's enthusiastic play and back to his mother as quickly as he could. Glamour, on the other hand, being part of an extended family which had Gizmo and Google, was made of sterner stuff.

Occasionally Glitter would turn up. Upon spotting her, Gizmo would joyously rush to her. Glitter would promptly sit down and groom him and carry him around. Gizmo loved being loved by Glitter. The bond between the two of them had strengthened ever since Gremlin had taken Glitter's baby.

It was evident from her size that Glitter was pregnant. As her pregnancy advanced she turned into a loner except for calling in on Gremlin occasionally. Then she disappeared for a few days and, in the dark of the night of 27 May, gave birth to a baby. Six days later she came out of hiding and that morning we found her with Golden. Whenever Glitter moved, Golden would follow. Glitter was apprehensive and wouldn't let Golden come within touching distance. Then Tarzan came along. Although Tarzan was only 12 and two years younger than Glitter, he was big. Glitter seemed torn. It was as if she wanted the two of them to know that she was still friends even though some fear for her baby kept her away from them. Finally she plucked up courage and allowed Golden to come near, presenting herself to Golden in a gesture of friendship. Golden quickly assured her that she had no designs on the newborn and the twins sealed their bond with the rare act of genital rubbing. Then they wandered off together with Tarzan following them: it was as if he wanted to enter their inner sanctum. Finally, he reassured first Glitter by grooming her briefly, and then Golden by a long and intense bout of grooming. He seemed to be signalling that they were, after all, long-standing friends. They accepted his presence and it was only then, in early afternoon, that Tarzan took time off to feed. For a 12-year-old, his behaviour had been remarkably restrained and mature. Glitter and Golden stayed together for the rest of the day and then made nests, side by side, for the night.

We had a good look at the baby when Glitter came to sit with us. As she groomed and turned the baby over, Fiona exclaimed that she was a girl. She also noted that her face looked a lot like Glamour's had when she was a tiny baby. As we watched, it became apparent that Glitter was loving every minute of having a baby of her own and fussing over her. I could only guess how much having a baby meant to her, and to every Kasekelian female. I thought of Gaia who had lost her babies on three occasions to Gremlin, and of Glitter when Gremlin took away Baby G, and

of Nasa, who was so desperate to conceive. It seems life for a Kasekelian female acquires a new meaning when she starts a family.

Glitter was deliberately avoiding Gremlin, but some day they would have to meet and that day came when Glitter's baby was ten days old. That morning we'd found Frodo and Tom feeding on mbula and songati fruits. After a while they were joined by Golden with baby Glamour and, in due course, they all descended to Kakombe valley to feed on palm nuts and mgweiza fruit. Later on, in the early afternoon, Gaia and Gremlin turned up with Gremlin's two kids and fed at some distance away from the others. It was wayward Gimli who found Frodo and Tom. Because of his fascination with big males, he stayed with Frodo, joining Tom in grooming him. As Frodo and Tom wandered off, Gimli – without a thought for Gremlin who was left behind – joined them. Meanwhile Gremlin wanted to move on and waited for Gimli to turn up and, as she waited, she was joined by Golden.

After about 15 minutes, at around four o' clock, we heard loud cries. Gremlin rushed towards the source of the sound where she was joined by Gaia. Frodo and Tom arrived and there was much activity centred on greeting Frodo and pampering him with grooming. Tom was completely ignored and he visibly felt left out as he sat to one side. Little Gizmo had rushed to greet Frodo who was delighted to see him and embraced him with his huge arms. Then, smiling softly, he played with Gizmo. After the game, Frodo groomed Gizmo thoroughly but gently. In the middle of it all, Gimli turned up with Glitter and her baby, Gossamer.

Glitter was very nervous, clearly apprehensive that Gremlin might snatch her baby girl. At first Gremlin ignored Glitter, but Gimli and Gizmo were far from indifferent. They kept on looking at Gossamer and Gizmo gingerly touched Gossamer's little hand. Gizmo had also missed his elder sister who hugged him and carried him up a tree to groom and fuss over him. When Glitter descended, she saw that the women and Frodo were engaged in grooming. Glitter sat to one side but, in due course, Gremlin inched towards Glitter and groomed her nervous daughter's back as Glitter held her baby in her crotch, shielding her. Nothing sinister transpired. Presently, Gremlin got up and crossed the Kakombe stream. It was then that Glitter followed, doubled back as Gremlin climbed a tree, and slunk off after Frodo and Tom who had gone in the opposite direction. She had reintroduced herself, with Gossamer, to Gremlin but also given Gremlin the slip, for now.

Glitter's motive in knowingly walking into potential danger wasn't difficult to decipher. Like many Kasekelians, she cannot live without strong group bonds. Whatever happened, the bond with her mother had to continue. She had to reintegrate herself into the family and the sooner she did it the better. She had started to get everyone used to the newest Kasekelian and also to minimise the danger of a Gremlin baby-snatch during those critical early days.

In early afternoon of the next day, Glitter turned up again. Gizmo spotted her at once and rushed to his favourite sister. There was a joyous reunion, as if they had not seen each other for weeks and Gimli, sensing fun, joined in too. It seemed to us that the entire G Dynasty appeared to lead very rich emotional lives. We sat and watched. Glitter was once again tentative around Gremlin but, in due course, Glitter and Gremlin groomed each other. Glitter relaxed and actually lay down to rest. But it was only for a couple of minutes. Jumpy, she sat up and walked off. Gremlin called her back and groomed her. Then Glitter again decided to go, whereupon she was followed by an eager Gizmo. Glitter told him not to follow but, while Gizmo obeyed, somewhat confused, Gremlin followed. They climbed a tree and fed and eventually Glitter managed to slip away, unnoticed.

Clearly Glitter was reintegrating into the family in small, spaced-out doses. She wanted Gremlin to get used to Gossamer and accept her within the family as Glitter's own. Her own bond with Gossamer was getting stronger with each passing day as she suckled and looked after her. Thus another baby snatch was avoided and Glitter was back in the G fold with a new addition.

Looking back, I reckon that we spent the most time with the G's, partly because they accepted our presence unconditionally. The time spent gave us a unique window through which we could watch the young G's growing up. I don't believe we found out anything new or made a major or even a minor discovery, but I do think it made us reassess our own way of living our family lives.

We saw Gossamer grow up amidst lots of love, and I must say that she loved in return. For Glitter, Gossamer was someone she could lavish vast affection on. It seemed to me that Glitter was meant to be a mother. There was no confusion in her mind, only certainty as to what she had to do – a fulfilment, perhaps, of an ancient imperative. She revealed a simple approach to mothering that was filled with quiet joy.

We saw Glamour grow up like a boy, often getting into three-way games with her older uncle Gizmo and older cousin Google and not flinching when play got out of hand. She was a tough girl with an upbringing full of love but also exposed to reality. All credit to Golden for letting Glamour be and for being there if Glamour needed her. Once again, we glimpsed an untainted childhood that was starkly honest and sincere.

The twins had clearly turned a corner. It had been touch and go – being physically small to start with, surviving hostile attacks from Fanni and Fifi, and being dependent on Gremlin to make history by bringing them up to adulthood. Despite Gremlin perversely setting Glitter back by snatching her first baby, the twins came through. Although they didn't rate high in the female hierarchy, they probably didn't care. What they did care about were their babies and, in Gossamer and Glamour, they had lively, healthy babies they could mother and feel complete with. Bliss can be simple to realise.

As for Gizmo, he was a source of concern in that his growing up seemed erratic. In October 2012 Gizmo was three years old whereas Glamour was only one. Yet, from afar we found it hard to distinguish between them by size. Gizmo was also moody; sometimes he joined in play and at other times he would stubbornly cling to Gremlin. He adored males and would, without hesitation, run up to Frodo, Faustino or Fudge to be hugged. Yet, even in his relationship with the big guys he was a puzzle. Once he saw Faustino and ran to him with obvious delight. But Faustino wasn't feeling well that day – he was sleeping a lot – and so didn't pay much attention to the little chap. Yet on another occasion, when Gizmo and

Faustino met up, Faustino invited him to play, a great privilege, but Gizmo simply clung on to Gremlin. Sometimes it seemd Gizmo was too dependent on Gremlin.

Gizmo's nephew, Google, was more forthright – bold, inquisitive, energetic and playful. He was also a fast learner who honed his instincts by watching and practising. We will not forget the day we saw Google watch the males display and then, in his little sheltered corner, display himself about 20 times, finally collapsing in a heap, exhausted for once. One influence on Google that may tell in the future is this: Gaia didn't take readily to big social gatherings, often staying on the sidelines with Google and so he missed out on novel social interactions.

Gaia herself was quiet, unhurried and self-contained. It would, however, be a mistake to think of her as being without emotions. We have seen her, after a temporary separation, greet the other G's joyously, hugging each one with obvious pleasure. She would get aggressive when any danger threatened Google but was generally well behaved and therefore not very exciting on the surface. Her mothering strategy – indeed, that of most Kasekelians – was to let her child grow at his own pace. Nothing was forced on Google, no competitive spirit induced. I just can't help but think that this is the most simple, clear and efficient mothering ploy in the long run.

Gimli's antics made us laugh, but his personality made us think. When, in the beginning, we encountered a seven-year-old Gimli, he was so sure of himself that he would get up to daring mischief like taunting male baboons. But Gremlin was always on hand should matters escalate, and if Gimli lost contact with Gremlin he would panic and whimper, desperately trying to reconnect with her. So the man of the G dynasty wasn't quite a man. A year later however, something had changed – perhaps some hormones had kicked in. He was being increasingly drawn to the big males and was following them almost single-mindedly. Gremlin, perhaps anxious because she knew that Gimli was inexperienced in the ways of the males, kept up with him as he roamed with his heroes. But the playful kid was growing up, getting interested in power and sex. Like it or not, growing up means change.

One day in October 2012, while returning to the rest house after a fruitless search for a group of Kasekelians led by the males, we came across the entire G dynasty. Gizmo and Google were playing, with Glamour joining in whenever she felt like playing too. Gimli was lying on his back, contemplating the sky. Golden was being nutty and Glitter was clutching Gossamer, studying us with fascination. Looking over all this was Gremlin. We could detect a smile of satisfaction playing on her face.

Whilst watching the G's chill out a thought struck me: the G's are atypical in a number of ways – their numerical strength for example – a consequence of Gaia, Golden and Glitter staying on. Furthermore, there is one peculiarity of the dynasty that has consequences for their status in the Kasekela Community. Out of nine of them, the eldest four are female and the youngest two are female as well. The three males in between are boys really. All hopes of leadership rest on young Gimli. Although transitioning, at nine years of age he's still a kid. So the G's are some way off from leadership of the Community. The S dynasty, on the other hand, has the potential to produce a candidate sooner.

Preceding page: Gremlin and Gimli. Currently,
Gremlin's family of children and grandchildren is
nine strong.

Gizmo riding on Gremlin as she makes her way
from one fruit tree to another. This was just
after Gizmo had put on a display of surprising
boldness. Gremlin and Samwise had been sitting
together in a bare tree, with three-year-old
Gizmo playing nearby. Suddenly, Samwise began
attacking Gremlin. Gremlin escaped and tried to
gather up Gizmo, who slipped by and, running
to Samwise, slapped her on the back as if to say
don't you dare attack my mother. He did it again
a few moments later.

Gizmo after being reunited with his mother. The previous day,
Gremlin and Gizmo had been separated after the males had got
excited and displayed. Immediately after their reunion, Gizmo spent
a long time suckling. After resting he then visibly perked up, taking
in his surroundings and playing a little by himself. Exploring a little,
he found a palm-nut fruit, all within a few metres of Gremlin. He
was clearly nervous about losing contact with her again.

Concerned Gimli watching Gremlin. In mid-2012 we
found that Gremlin was resting a lot and moving less,
as if physical exertion easily tired her. We thought that
old age was catching up with her, but we were wrong.
Later that year, she roamed tirelessly with the males.
Perhaps back then she had been shaking off a viral
infection. If so, it stayed with her for a long time.

Gizmo and Gimli play. A change had come over
little Gizmo since the death of Baby G. He was more
active, less brooding. He kept close to Gremlin, but
when Gremlin settled down for a long rest, Gizmo
played with his elder brother Gimli – or was it a case
of Gimli playing with Gizmo?

G family antics. Once, when Gaia and Google joined up with Gremlin, the two adults spent ages patiently fishing for termites. At first the kids joined in, but they quickly got bored and gave up. They turned to play which threatened to get out of hand when Gimli piled in. Then Gimli lost interest and sat, assuming his serious thinking pose, freeing up the kids to play by themselves.

Nyota and Duke. Nuru's 20-month-old baby boy, Nyota,
wanted to play with Dilly's 10-month-old baby boy, Duke. Duke
got frightened whenever Nyota tried to play with him, and he
would quickly retreat to mummy.

Gizmo and Glamour. Golden and Glamour would also drop in on Gremlin. Although only nine months old, Glamour showed none of Duke's fear in her play with Gizmo, often giving back as good a thump or friendly bite as she got. She seemed happy to be in the thick of rough and tumble. Golden hardly ever intervened and Gremlin turned a blind eye.

Glitter with her baby, six-day-old Gossamer. You could see in the tender way Glitter groomed Gossamer that having a baby meant a lot to her. Glitter was also protective of Gossamer. Once, three-and-a-half-month-old Gossamer attempted to climb a small bush and Glitter placed a hand under her body, encouraging her to climb but also providing a safety net. Gossamer was highly active but had not yet mastered coordination.

Tarzan (above) and Golden (right). Tarzan looks a lot like Golden, which isn't surprising since they have the same father – Frodo. Furthermore, the difference in age between them is small, only a year and three months. What's delightful is that their mothers were good friends, as are Tarzan and Golden themselves.

Gossamer being herself. At three and a half months
old, Gossamer not only looks like Baby G but also
wriggles like her, eyes wide open, trying to see
everything going on around her.

The G's get down to some serious grooming. From left to right: little Glamour, Golden, Gremlin and Gimli, lying down. The G's were often ranging in Kakombe valley which has a good supply of food, especially the rich palm-nut fruit. They could thus afford to take time off for socialising.

Gimli and the G family. Gimli, in the foreground, is
up to his antics again. In the background, from left
to right: Gizmo, Gremlin and Golden with Glamour
holding on to Golden. Gimli was often at a loose end.
He had energy to spare but often no one of his age
to play with. When the adults wanted to rest but he
wanted to go, he would get frustrated and sit apart,
often with a bored expression on his face.

Glamour at nine months. It's not clear whether she is flipping her upper lip out of habit or is fascinated by her ability to do it and so keeps on doing it every now and then. Watching Glamour for a long period, I got the impression that she had an urge to be active and to exercise her brain at every opportunity, and this is perhaps the reason why she comes across as being inventive. She is also bold; she started chasing baboons at two months of age.

Glamour at two years and two months. Her urge to be active has abated only a little. At times, when she sits and ponders for a few seconds, you can glimpse what she could look like when grown up.

A transfixed Glitter holding Gossamer. On her right is Google, and behind him is Glamour. Glitter, every now and then, appears to lose herself in thought.

Golden, who just can't help behaving in a peculiarly Golden manner. She still manages to get her way with Gremlin too. Once, when the G's were termite-fishing, Gremlin went looking for a vine and returned with a large one. Golden saw it and asked for it by grabbing it. Gremlin held on to it, refusing to give it to Golden. Golden held on and pleaded whereupon Gremlin broke the vine in two and gave Golden a piece.

One big happy, chilled-out dynasty. Gremlin, on the right, looks on, with Google next, while Glamour and Gizmo seem to be arguing. Then there's Gossamer holding Golden's leg while Golden herself is being groomed by Glitter. Not in the picture are Gaia, sitting close by, and Gimli, happily foraging in a tree. All the nine G's had been moving down to the lake from high up when they decided to take a break.

Glitter with Gossamer on the left, and Golden with
Glamour on the right. By having babies themselves,
the twins have gone down in history. We often
found the twins together with their babies. Golden
and Glitter had always been close, but since they
had babies they have been bound closer than
before. Being the same age, they shared many
similar experiences in the past and are now sharing
another important one.

Chapter 8: **The Rise of the S Dynasty**

The S dynasty can be traced back to that remarkable old girl, Sparrow. Although she is estimated to be 54, which is very old, she acts young – still, for example, scaling tall trees with agility. She also has a taste for meat. In fact, it turns out that the S dynasty is more carnivorous than the other dynasties in Kasekela.

Whenever the Kasekelians come across colobus monkeys in tall trees, Sparrow urges the males to have a go. Once she got so excited, yelling in Ferdinand's face as she urged him to begin hunting, that he lost his cool and slapped her. Happily, Sparrow held his face in apology five minutes later and he accepted.

We saw the Kasekelians hunt colobus monkeys several times, but there was one stand-out incident in which six colobus monkeys were taken down. Just beyond the first mango tree in the south, a troop of red colobus was resting in a tree. It was spotted by the group of 37 Kasekelians we were with and they began stalking them. Samwise, the 11-year-old daughter of Sandi and granddaughter of Sparrow, climbed up the tree and chased them. The tree was some distance from an adjoining tree and, by displaying at the monkeys, Samwise was able to create a panic which led to the frightened monkeys trying to leap to the safety of the next tree. However, because of the large gap between the trees, a few couldn't make it and fell to the ground 30 metres below. On cue, the Kasekelians dashed through the undergrowth while we followed them at a crawling pace. We found that they had captured several monkeys. In fact, an adult colobus with a broken leg was surrounded by Kasekelians who didn't bother to kill it for several hours while they feasted noisily on the other captured monkeys.

More monkeys appeared in the trees several hours later, and members of the S dynasty had another go – Sandi in the lead with Sampson following and Sparrow bringing up the rear. Sampson climbed the tree fast and managed to grab the tail of an adult female. In the ensuing struggle she fell to the ground. Hurt, she couldn't move. Several Kasekelians surrounded her and Sampson finally grabbed her head and bashed it to the ground. Fudge finished the job and Sampson shared the meat among his peers, giving the bulk of it to Fudge.

Currently Sparrow has two sons, Sheldon and Sinbad, and two daughters, Sandi and Schweini, living in Kasekela. Schweini has tried to emigrate to Mitumba. To execute a successful emigration, a female should venture into foreign land when she is most receptive to the males there – she needs protection from the females. Schweini first attempted to emigrate to Mitumba in February 2004. She was attacked vehemently by the Mitumba females and returned in a terrible state to Kasekela. She tried to emigrate again in October 2005 but was again attacked by the local females and forced to return. The mistake Schweini made was that she attempted to emigrate when she wasn't at the stage in her cycle most attractive to males. Consequently, the Mitumba males only made half-hearted attempts to shield her from the fierce attacks of the females.

Schweini stayed on in Kasekela after that and gave birth to a baby in September 2007. The baby didn't survive but Schweini gave birth again in 2009 to a girl called Safi. When we saw Safi that June 2011, she came across as a lively two-year-old, a delight to see. Then Safi met with an accident.

Once again, Schweini had gone north toward Mitumba, this time with Safi. After a day or so she was seen at the border with wounds over her body, although Safi looked okay. The next time Schweini was seen, she was alone and looking worse and eventually she made her way back to Kasekela. Safi has never been seen again. Schweini hung around with her friend Rumumba, a young immigrant female who came into Kasekela Community in around 2010 from Mitumba. When Rumumba wasn't around, Schweini travelled with her elder sister Sandi and made a slow but sure recovery.

In November 2012, a few weeks after we had left, Schweini gave birth to a boy, Shwali, and so far mother and baby are doing well. We saw Schweini and Shwali in September 2013 and he was a handful. Only ten months old, he was constantly playing, climbing trees and exploring. Schweini had resigned herself to his tirelessness. She kept an eye on him and let him be.

With Shwali the S dynasty became nine-strong. It used to be a periphery dynasty. The matriarch, Sparrow, didn't interact much with the other Kasekelians and largely kept to her corner of the Community's range. Things have begun to change, however. Sandi and her three children, as well as her younger sister Schweini, have been finding themselves in the middle of social gatherings. Sandi's rank and status was high and moving up, and Ferdinand had a crush on Sandi and she knew it.

One day we heard loud calls from above Kakombe valley and, heading towards them, we found Ferdinand with Sandi and her family – Sampson, Siri and Samwise – and six other Kasekelians. Ferdinand was very attentive and friendly toward Sandi. He was clearly courting her. He was also in a belligerent mood, demonstrating to the gathered Kasekelians that Sandi was his and woe betide anyone who should forget it.

I was intrigued by Ferdinand's behaviour. Five-year-old Siri was still suckling, indicating that Sandi might not have been quite ready to have another child. On the other hand, mothers such as Fifi and Fanni had given birth while their dependent children were still not weaned. Did Ferdinand know that Sandi was ready? For an undisputed leader who should have no difficulty in impressing girls, he was going out of his way to court Sandi assiduously. Later that day we saw something surprising. Ferdinand and Sandi and Siri were sitting on the ground and Ferdinand looked up and saw some tasty vines. He climbed up and then called Sandi to share the vine source. She called back and climbed up. Siri stayed behind. The two adults vocalised softly as they ate. It was a lovely sharing moment. I would like to stick my neck out and suggest that Ferdinand was thinking long term. Not only did Sandi have a good record of bearing and rearing children, but she also had 12-year-old Samwise accompanying her. Samwise then wasn't quite ready to bear children, but it wouldn't be much longer. Intelligent courtship perhaps pays.

Turning to the S males, there were 30-year-old Sheldon, 17-year-old Sampson, 12-year-old Sinbad and six-year-old Siri. Sheldon, a former leader with a still-powerful build, didn't seem interested in climbing back to the top of the hierarchy. So the only candidate who could bid for the leadership was Sampson who was too respectful of the F boys. His best chance would lie in forming an alliance with elder brother Sheldon and then taking on the F boys. But that hasn't happened so far and so the F's shouldn't feel threatened by the S dynasty – not yet anyway.

S family portrait. From left to right: Fudge (son of Sheldon), Schweini with baby Shwali, Sampson looking down, Sparrow looking up and a chilled-out Sinbad. It was early morning on a cloudy day and the S family members, having met up with Fudge, set about bonding with him. The S's are a tight-knit family who retain their separate identity even when within a big group of Kasekelians.

An excited Sparrow nagging an indifferent Frodo. There are colobus monkeys in a nearby tree and Sparrow is yelling in Frodo's face to have a go at catching them. Frodo ignores her, however. It's not that Frodo doesn't love meat, but rather that with old age has come a loss of speed and agility, both essential for catching fast-moving monkeys in treetops.

Sparrow. The oldest Kasekelian and the matriarch of the large S Dynasty, Sparrow is high-ranking and also has an endearing habit of keeping out of trouble when males display. At such an event we find her crouched but watchful. Like all members of the S Dynasty, her one weakness is a love of meat. All in all, Sparrow is quite a unique lady.

Twelve-year-old Samwise, daughter of Sandi and Frodo. She still travels with Sandi but otherwise can be quite bold. We once saw her chasing colobus monkeys on thin branches high up, moving as quickly as the panic-stricken monkeys. In addition to her physical prowess, we have seen her make ingenious use of sticks to create tools.

Sinbad, accompanied by Sparrow, moving with the
males. Sinbad seems to have inherited his father
Frodo's bulk. Emotionally, he is firmly attached to
his mother and has yet to show signs of striking out
on his own, thereby making the transition to being
an independent male.

Sinbad. Eleven-year-old Sinbad is quite a family guy, always
pleased when elder brother, Sheldon and elder sisters, Sandi
and Schweini drop by. His relationship with his niece, Samwise,
whom he is generally fond of, has been erratic, because a
testosterone surge can make him quite aggressive towards
her. As yet, Sinbad is not ranked in the male hierarchy.

Schweini. Younger sister of Sandi, 21-year-old
Schweini has had a troubled history since reaching
adulthood. Twice she was beaten back to Kasekela
by Mitumba females when she tried to emigrate to
their Community. Then she gave birth to her first
baby but soon after lost it, cause unknown.

Safi. Two-year-old Safi was Schweini's second baby.
She looked alert, healthy and playful when we
spent some time with her and Schweini in 2011.
Both continued to do well until Schweini tried to
emigrate once again to Mitumba. She was beaten
back yet again and returned to Kasekela minus Safi,
now presumed dead.

Rumumba. 14-year-old Rumumba is an immigrant
female from the Mitumba Community to the north.
Shy and servile, she seems aware of her peripheral
position in social gatherings. She often wanders on
her own but attracts the males when she is sexually
receptive. She is at the stage in her life when she is
ready to start a family.

Schweini, fully recovered. Schweini had returned
to Kasekela badly injured and mentally shaken
after her failed third attempt to emigrate. She
alternated between hanging around with
her elder sister Sandi and her young friend
Rumumba as she slowly recovered.

Schweini and Shwali on the move. Schweini gave birth to a baby boy, Shwali, in November 2012. We first glimpsed them in September the following year and found that Schweini was very relaxed and that 10-month-old Shwali had adapted several styles of riding on mum. Over time, we also discovered that Shwali was very active and observant, often fighting sleep in order to take in all that was happening around him.

Sandi. Sparrow's eldest offspring, Sandi is now a high-ranking female, evidence that the S family has risen from nothing to a dominant position. When Sparrow came in as an immigrant, she was shy and on the periphery. But she was fertile. She raised children to maturity and conferred her rising status on them.

Ferdinand puffed up. When Ferdinand was courting Sandi he would occasionally display, all fluffed up, at the other Kasekelians. It was his way of telling them to keep off Sandi. Ferdinand's attention to Sandi was unwavering. There were a couple of other females keen to attract his attention but Ferdinand ignored them. To please Sandi, he even condescended to play with her boy, Siri.

Schweini and Shwali. Having Shwali has changed
Schweini's demeanour. She mixes freely with all
the Kasekelian females but, out of a concern for
Shwali, keeps away from the big males. She moves
with grace and when resting wears an expression
of quiet pleasure on her face, as if transformed by
having attained a purpose in life.

Shwali. He is only 10 months old in the picture but looks much older. He is actually quite advanced for his age and that, together with being a member of a large dynasty, bodes well for him in the future.

Chapter 9: **The Minor Dynasties and the Immigrants**

For the Kasekelians, as for every living group, life follows death. Consider the following natural phenomenon. 33-year-old Zrezia gave birth to a baby just a few days before Glitter had Baby G. And a few days after Gremlin took Baby G from Glitter, Zrezia's baby died. Now here is the odd thing: after nine weeks had elapsed both Zrezia and Glitter became sexually receptive almost simultaneously. Actually, Zrezia was continuing a small dynasty which was started by her mother and which also had a link with the G dynasty.

First, a little look at Zrezia's past. A long time ago, Zrusha, a stranger from the south, appeared at Kasekela. She stayed on and gave birth to Zrezia in 1978, and thus began the Z dynasty. Being an immigrant, Zrusha was low-ranking and Zrezia inherited her mother's status. Zrezia stayed on the periphery at social gatherings, trying not to be noticed by high-ranking females and deferring to them if chance brought them together. However, she had no problems with the males, who were most interested in her when she was at her most attractive sexually. She also succeeded in ingratiating herself with the powerful F dynasty. At that time, Freud was the leader and Frodo was rising in rank. Frodo was terribly interested in sex and, taking advantage of Freud's absences from the centre of Kasekela, he courted Zrezia and the result was Zeus, born in January 1995.

We first encountered Zeus when we walked south along the lake's beach one September morning in 2011. It was a pleasant walk out in the open, with the soothing rhythm of the waves caressing the beach and the rising sun blocked behind the hills to the east. We cut into the forest after an hour and found a group of Kasekelians, with Zeus sitting at the edge of the group. He was 17 and seemed to have inherited Frodo's bulk and Zrezia's unassuming nature. Unlike Fudge, who

gave in to his testosterone surges by displaying, Zeus stayed quietly in the background. He spent time with the big males but always with an unerring sense of his place in an all-male group. We noticed that whenever Ferdinand came near him, Zeus cringed or quickly scurried away. He gave the strong impression that he could never start an uprising against Ferdinand.

When Zeus wasn't with the males, he was with Zrezia and his younger sister, Zella. Zrezia had become pregnant when she had got together with the then high-ranking Kris and Zella, born in November 1999, was the result. Whenever we encountered Zella, we thought she looked slim and charming. She is a mummy's girl too and, in keeping with the character of the Z dynasty, stays in the background when big social gatherings occur, quietly watching the main players and ready to flee to safety should a male give in to a testosterone surge.

I distinctly remember the day we first saw the entire Z dynasty – Zrezia, Zeus, Zella and five-year-old Zinda – in the southern part of the Community's range in September 2011. The little boy was the highlight – bouncy and playful. It is, in fact, Zinda who links the Z dynasty with the G dynasty. Zinda is one of the two legacies of Gimble, the younger brother of Gremlin. When Gimble was 29 years old and had settled into the role of a high ranking male, with all his unsuccessful attempts at the leadership behind him, he had courted Zrezia assiduously and Zinda was the result.

We were back in Kasekela in May 2012, and one evening when Fiona and I were walking back to the rest house through the forest, Fiona heard a rustling sound. On investigation, which involved crawling into the undergrowth – the April rains had brought about such vigorous growth that the forest was thicker than ever before – we found six-year-old Zinda and big male Faustino feeding on vines. Zrezia, Zinda's mother, was nowhere to be seen. Puzzled, we probed into Zinda's recent history back at the rest house. It turned out that Zinda was a plucky little boy who had a mind of his own and wandered about the forest alone or in the company of a male. He had been with Faustino for at least six days, roaming the forest with him. How he kept up with the fast-moving male is a mystery.

Of course, Zinda was very brave. He was only six, yet so different from other youngsters older than him. For example, we witnessed a scene in which eight-year-old Gimli had lingered behind and got separated from his mother, Gremlin, who had climbed into a tree some 50 yards away. Gimli was distressed, crying softly until he was reunited. Then there was the brief episode when 12-year-old Fundi got separated from elder brother Fudge in a melee caused by Titan charging in to impress the girls. Fundi went around looking for his brother, crying and sobbing. He also let out one big scream, but no Fudge appeared. Then he spotted Titan in a tall tree and eagerly climbed up, and all was well in his little world. By way of contrast, the only occasions on which we saw Zinda betray insecurity was whenever Faustino climbed a tree too tall for him to scale. He would then beg Faustino not to climb. Of course, Faustino paid no attention to Zinda's pleas. So Zinda would cut a forlorn figure as he waited under the tree for Faustino to climb down.

The next day Faustino met up with Frodo and Zinda transferred allegiance to him. Together they roamed for three days. Frodo was more attentive to Zinda, waiting for the frantic little figure to catch up whenever he got left behind. The next morning, Frodo met up with Ferdinand. The three fed together and when Ferdinand set out on his own, Zinda accompanied him. Zinda was quite chuffed at being in the company of the leader and dutifully groomed Ferdinand as best he could whenever they rested together. It seemed that Zinda didn't care who he was travelling with as long as it was an adult male.

When we returned to Kasekela three months later, we kept a lookout for the Z family. Zeus, the 18-year-old eldest son of Zresia, looked in good shape. But he hadn't made much progress in climbing the male hierarchy. He hung back when the males were around and rarely plucked up courage to join their grooming sessions. Despite being big and impressive when he displayed, Zeus seemed to lack the mental strength to take on the other males in one-to-one situations. However, he does display at the females when the males are not around and causes panic among them.

I can recall one incident with great clarity when Zeus showed his prowess. We had climbed up high with a little difficulty, following a large group led by the males. They rested around midday at a crest from where we had a good view of the lake in the distance. After a while, the males moved on, leaving Zeus self-grooming under a tree. Nearby, the G Dynasty was resting and grooming when Nasa passed by. Gizmo ran to her to be cuddled and groomed; apparently Nasa has a soft spot for him and vice versa. After a while, with no other male in sight, Zeus displayed, charging through the girls and the kids, roughly pushing a bewildered Google out of his way. Nasa at once took Gizmo to safety as Gremlin ran away from Zeus. Later, Gremlin and Gizmo were reunited.

During this visit a new baby was born in Kasekela. On the night of 7 October, 23-year-old Tanga gave birth to her third child. The next morning, we came across Tanga and saw Sparrow closing in on her. Tanga edged back as Sparrow moved forward, reaching out to the baby. Tanga kept retreating until she reached a tree and climbed into it. Sparrow followed and once again reached for the baby held closely to Tanga's chest. Tanga climbed farther up and squealed repeatedly. Just then, Frodo chanced by and came to Tanga's aid by charging and putting a stop to Sparrow's advance. Then Sheldon came along and when he moved on Sparrow accompanied her son. Was Sparrow just curious or did she have meat on her mind?

Tanga spent the rest of the day in the intermittent company of Frodo and constant company of her son Tom and daughter Tabora, both of whom seemed to know that a significant event had occurred in their little family. Tarzan, Tanga's younger brother, was highly interested too, but Titan betrayed no curiosity towards the new arrival. To be sure, Tanga and Titan used to play a lot when Titan was a kid, but lately the brother-sister pair didn't appear to interact much. I wondered if this was short-sighted on Titan's part, because Titan could have done with strong family backing if he ever decides to take Ferdinand and Faustino on for the leadership.

Over the next few months, the quartet of Tanga, Tom, Tabora and baby Tarime wandered together. When we next saw them, about seven months later, Tarime appeared alert, curious and quite content to cling to Tanga or play close to Tanga when Tanga was resting. She looked very cute, and Tom adored his little sister. It all looked quaint, but when Tarime was 10 months old an unimaginable incident occurred.

That day Tanga was grooming Ferdinand, who was lying on the ground. Tarime was playing by herself near the pair and Tom and Tabora were some distance away. Ferdinand got up, grabbed Tarime and ran off with her, followed by a panic-stricken, defecating Tanga. Tom, clearly distraught, followed. Ferdinand shot up a tree, killed Tarime and started eating her. The bizarre thing was that a little later Tanga and Tabora joined in the gruesome feast. Only Tom kept away, highly agitated, comprehending what had happened but unable to act. What was going through Ferdinand's mind when he snatched Tarime and through Tanga's mind when she joined in eating her own baby? There does not seem to be an obvious reason for this behaviour.

In the past in Kasekela, there has only been one known incident of male infanticide. That happened when Freud killed Tofiki, infant son of Tita and grandson of Tatti. But Freud didn't cannibalise. Such incidents are difficult to understand. No amount of observation and analysis is going to access the workings of the minds of Freud and Ferdinand. These are unchartered territories. It was also the third known instance of cannibalism at Kasekela. I'll describe the second shortly.

We also received news of Eliza, one of the periphery females who had emigrated from the Kalande Community to Kasekela years earlier. Erick, her first son, was doing fine and was already four years old, though not quite weaned. Eliza and Erick were a self-contained pair, usually on their own but occasionally joining the others. Then Erick would play a lot with whichever youngsters were around while Eliza engaged in a grooming session with the adults. We had grown quite fond of the pair and so were pleased to hear that Eliza had given birth to her second baby in late August 2012.

Soon after the birth, Eliza, Erick and the baby were travelling on a trail when Sampson came by. Further up the trail, Ferdinand was courting Sandi. Ferdinand was only cursorily interested in Eliza's newborn. As they moved further up the trail, Faustino suddenly appeared and displayed at Eliza. She panicked and ran to Ferdinand and Sandi for protection. Unfortunately, Ferdinand joined in with Faustino in beating up Eliza as did Sampson. In desperation, Eliza edged near Sandi who saw the baby, took it and ate it as the males continued to pound Eliza. Sandi ranks higher than Eliza and had the backing of the two top-ranking males, Ferdinand and Faustino, as well as the entire S dynasty, including her son Sampson. There was nothing Eliza could have done that wouldn't have been futile. No one can tell what was going on in the males' minds or in Sandi's mind either. You can only guess. It's possible that Sandi is simply partial to meat and saw an opportunity to indulge herself.

Eliza herself wasn't badly hurt and, after the tragedy, retired to safety with her son Erick. In the days that followed she was quite affectionate towards Erick and watched over him diligently until, that is, she resumed her cycle. It was a changed Eliza then, soliciting any male who would mate with her, including even eight-year-old Gimli.

Gimli was playing a game that involved going round and round a tree with Sandi's son, Siri. Just then Eliza came and waved her bottom in Gimli's face, whereupon Siri left. So Gimli was going round the tree backwards, obviously enjoying a new variation on an old game, with Eliza moving backwards as well, trying to press her bottom in his face. In due course, Gimli realised that this wasn't a new game and that Eliza wanted to mate with him. He duly obliged.

Eliza was found to be pregnant in January 2013. In keeping with her new state, she was travelling alone and taking long naps. Unfortunately, another pregnancy test administered in July found that she was no longer pregnant. She started becoming sexually attractive again and in September to October was Ferdinand's girl. He kept a close eye on her, mated with her and then left her when she was no longer sexually attractive.

Eliza's new-found enthusiasm for having a baby meant that she began to neglect Erick. When in a mating mood, she would leave a bewildered-looking Erick behind and go searching for males in the vicinity. Erick would just lie on the ground, looking rather sorry for himself and waiting for Eliza to return. Clearly, she had misplaced her maternal instinct for Erick, and the distance between the mother and her four-year-old son widened to a point where it would never close. Erick spent more and more time on his own and then quietly disappeared from the scene forever.

Eliza's arrival as an immigrant was part of a general drift of immigrant females to Kasekela from the southern Community of Kalande. That Community was in disarray with only one mature male left. No wonder the females were leaving.

One of them was Nasa, a big 24-year-old female who immigrated to the Kasekela Community in 2000.

We first saw Nasa when she was with Faustino and had sex on her mind, but Faustino, although pleased with the grooming she was giving him, wasn't in a mood for mating. On the third day of their being together, the couple met up with Pax. After a few minutes we saw an annoyed Nasa attack and chase a bewildered Pax, who ran for his life. The reason for the attack was a mystery. That a female, albeit a big one, is capable of dominating Pax just showed how low he was in the rankings. Of course, the presence of Faustino may have emboldened Nasa, but it seems that Nasa knew that Pax was a pushover. However, Pax and Nasa may have something in common.

It was puzzling that Nasa was yet to have a baby. Perhaps, just as Pax is impotent, Nasa is infertile. On the other hand, there is a strange phenomenon associated with immigrant females. Consider Vanilla who hangs about in the southern part of the Kasekela Community's range and rarely ventures further north. She feels secure like that. She most likely emigrated from Kalande Community to Kasekela in about 2000. She was alone then and remained childless for a good many years, giving the impression that she was infertile. But then in 2010, at the age of 22, she gave birth to a boy, Victor. Two years later, both mother and son were afflicted with a skin disease involving almost complete loss of hair. Victor died but Vanilla made a slow recovery, although today she looks prematurely aged.

Another such female is Nuru. She, too, was thought to be infertile when she first arrived as an immigrant. But then, at the age of 20, she gave birth to Nyota. Another immigrant from the south, Imani, was also late in giving birth. At the age of 17, a boy, Ipo, was born. By way of comparison with the resident females, Fifi had Freud when she was 13, Fanni had Fax when she was 11 and Gremlin had Getty when she was 12.

Perhaps the process of integrating into the host community delays conception. It seems that the first priority of a nervous female is to avoid getting beaten up by the resident females, jealously guarding their scarce food resources. Then, having escaped the wrath of the incumbent females, usually though not always by seeking the protection of a male, the immigrant tries to become assimilated into her new society. This takes time and is fraught with uncertainty, which is perhaps why any conception is delayed. It's only when she is sure that she has been accepted in the community that she can look forward to having a baby.

There are several avenues to integration. One immigrant female, 23-year-old Bahati, ingratiated herself with the S dynasty when she first came. Since the S dynasty tended to keep apart from the others, she was able to integrate well with them and settle down quickly. When Nasa came, she banded with other immigrants and took time to be accepted by the powerful dynasties. However, later on she went for the bold strategy of doggedly following Faustino and Ferdinand and soliciting them for mating. She is now accepted as a bona fide member of the Community but has yet to have a baby, and she is already 24, hence the possibility that she is barren.

Another female I remember very well is Skosha. When she was in her teens, the males would gather round her and pay her a lot of attention whenever she was sexually receptive. But when it gradually transpired that she was infertile, they ignored her. Not being able to raise a family must have been heart-breaking for Skosha. She passed her time hanging around with the other females, but although she was tolerated, she was ignored most of the time. Life became very lonely for her and, when she mysteriously disappeared, no one appeared to notice.

Another who disappeared was Beethoven. I first saw him during my very first visit to Kasekela; he was grooming Freud with his head tilted away from me. But when he moved his head up to scratch his own arm, I got a good look at his face and it seemed so appropriate to call him Beethoven. My curiosity was aroused and I dug up details of his past. Beethoven had joined the Community in December 1973 at the age of four. He had arrived unexpectedly with his nine-year-old sister, Harmony – their mother presumed dead. Beethoven then was a serious little chap who hardly played. He was also small and took longer than normal to reach adult size. Thereafter he rose steadily in rank. The high point of his ascendancy was the occasion when he challenged Wilkie for leadership and was defeated. After that he settled into a niche and didn't bother about climbing the hierarchy further, content to be just one of the boys. He tended to avoid the high-ranking males and evolved into a cool guy, keeping out of trouble.

Alas for Beethoven, the ailment that struck the Community towards the end of 2002 affected him badly. All the afflicted Kasekelians recovered except Beethoven, then aged 33. He was last seen in November 2002, wasted away. But he did leave behind a daughter, Dilly, whose face bears an uncanny likeness to his. Today, Dilly goes about in Kasekela with her seven-year-old daughter Diaz and two-year-old son, Duke. Sometimes when I glimpse Dilly I have to do a double-take to make sure Beethoven hasn't come back.

Following pages: Tanga resting on a tree high up in Kahama valley. Tanga had lost her baby, Tarime, and was sexually receptive again. For the moment she was avoiding attention from the males, especially the young males such as Sampson and Fundi, who were persistently following her and requesting mating. A few days later, Tanga was ready to be courted and cautiously started trying to attract the attention of the older males.

Zella. When we came across Zella, daughter of Zrezia and Kris, the then 11-year-old looked slim and charming. In keeping with the low status of her mother, she deferred to all adult Kasekelians. We had planned to get to know her better but didn't get the chance – Zella succumbed to a fatal illness when she was nearly 13 and on the verge of starting a family of her own.

Zrezia. At 34, Zrezia is a low-ranking female who
has inherited her lowly status from her immigrant
mother. To locate Zrezia when a large group has
formed, you need to cast your eye away from the
centre and scan the periphery. Most likely Zrezia
will be skulking there, sometimes with her son,
Zeus. Zrezia personifies wariness.

Zeus, the son of Zrezia and Frodo, 17-year-old Zeus is large in size but small in self-belief. He regards the likes of Ferdinand, Faustino and Titan with apprehension, hardly ever venturing near them. Perhaps having a nervous mother has not helped his confidence. Not surprisingly, he is currently of low rank.

Fundi at 12. Then, he still felt vulnerable when he was on his own. A year later, he would be following elder brother Fudge to such a degree that if you spotted Fudge you were bound to find Fundi by looking around. By then Fundi had gained in confidence by watching Fudge assert himself in the big male world. Often he rallied behind Fudge when Fudge displayed.

Gimli at eight. Gimli yearned to be a big male but he was still a mummy's boy. Whenever he was separated from his mother, he quickly became distressed and called to re-establish contact. Gremlin, perceiving her son's need to be near the big males, often travelled with a group of them, enabling a mesmerised Gimli to watch them in action.

Siri and Faustino sharing mshaishai. Big male Faustino is very tolerant of youngsters and sometimes plays with them. When in a benevolent mood, he even shares fruit with them. In this instance Faustino was able to reach up and pluck a bunch of tasty looking mshaishai. Siri noticed and, correctly reading Faustino's mood, cautiously edged nearer to him and managed to get a share.

Zinda and Ferdinand. Six-year-old Zinda was an
intrepid lad. He habitually left his mother, Zrezia,
and wandered off in the company of the big males.
He was quite chuffed when Ferdinand allowed him
to travel alongside, and he dutifully and eagerly
groomed the leader whenever they rested together.

Tanga walking with newborn baby (right) and the baby instinctively clinging tight to her (above). Tanga had given birth to Tarime earlier that morning. Invariably others came to have a look, but Frodo sensed Tanga's nervousness and scattered the onlookers. Tanga latched on to Frodo, who understood her need to be near him, and she followed him assiduously throughout the rest of the day.

Adolescent Tom being groomed by his mother, Tanga. Tom was a dwarf compared to others of a similar age although, with his crinkled, serious face, he gave the impression of deep maturity. Tom was a healthy, social and playful toddler, and there was no hint that he would not grow normally. His current small size places him at a disadvantage – even Gimli can bully him, despite Tom being three years older.

257

Tabora termite-fishing. Tom's younger sister,
Tabora, uses energy extravagantly. Yet when she
does something absorbing, such as fishing for
termites, she can be very patient. Focussed, she
spent an hour at this termite mound, catching a
lot of termites and eating them. While she was at
it, Titan passed by, made perfunctory attempts at
fishing, gave up and moved on.

Tarime, Tanga's baby, at seven months of age.
When Tarime was 10 months old, she was grabbed
by Ferdinand who then proceeded to kill and eat her.
More perplexingly, Tanga and Tabora joined in. The
only one who seemed distressed was Tom. As yet,
there is no explanation for this aberrant behaviour.

Nasa carrying a red colobus monkey that she
hunted on her own. She is hurrying on to get away
from other Kasekelians, who were bound to ask
for a share. On this occasion she refused to share
the meat with any of the males but did share it with
a few females. On another occasion she killed a
baboon and shared it with Ferdinand.

Nasa. Nasa is a striking-looking large female, almost
as big as Ferdinand. She comes across as being
very determined and decisive.

Pax waiting. Pax, 34, is waiting for pieces of meat to drop down from the tree above, where Kasekelians are feeding on a baboon. We have never seen Pax actively involved in a hunt. Quite often hunts involve a group of Kasekelians, predominantly male, and should Pax catch a monkey he would be robbed. So he settles for scraps.

Nasa aged 24. Nasa is high-ranking amongst the immigrants and she also mixes freely with the big males. She has yet to have a baby despite repeated attempts.

Nuru. At 22, Nuru is a striking-looking immigrant female. She gave birth to her first baby, Nyota, at the late age of 20. Nuru herself is very timid, but that doesn't deter Nyota from joining in any social gathering with gusto. They are a contrasting pair in temperament.

Vanilla. A 25-year-old immigrant, she's dipping for army ants. These ants are in a hard-to-reach underground nest, but Vanilla provoked them into attacking a stick by poking them with it. She then withdrew the stick, brushed them off it and put them in her mouth, eating very fast. The ants have a painful bite, and the long stick enabled Vanilla to keep her legs well clear of them while fishing.

Eliza and Sinbad. Eliza is soliciting mating from young
Sinbad, who pretends to be uninterested since several big
males are around. Sparrow is a spectator. As soon as the
other males departed, Sinbad was quick to mate with Eliza.

Erick aged four. We didn't get to know Erick well since
encounters with him and his mother, Eliza, were infrequent.
From what little we saw of him, he came across as normal
and well adjusted. But then, when his mother went through
a sex-obsessed phase and neglected him, he became
withdrawn and possibly depressed. He then disappeared,
never to be seen again.

Bahati (left) and Baseke (below left). Bahati, 23, is another female immigrant. She is well settled in Kasekela and has a sweet and very confident two-year-old daughter called Baseke. Bahati is on very good terms with Sparrow and the rest of the S family. When she first arrived in Kasekela, she ingratiated herself with them.

Imani (right) and Ipo (left). Imani emigrated from the Kalande Community in the south and was followed by her younger sister, Iowyn. The two sisters are still very close. Like Nuru, Imani gave birth to a baby boy, called Ipo, at a late age. Like Nuru again, she is socially timid, whereas Ipo, like Nuru's boy Nyota, is bold.

Beethoven, aged 33. Males don't usually migrate, but Beethoven did. At the age of four, Beethoven arrived unexpectedly in Kasekela with his elder sister Harmony. It's almost certain that they were orphans. Because Beethoven was perceived to be harmless and his sister had the protection of the males, he was left alone. He did quite well, his high point being to challenge Wilkie for leadership. Defeated, he gave up politics.

Apollo (left) and Dilly (middle). They are at Hilltop, a relatively open area reached after a long climb. The Kasekelians have fed and are resting, the early-morning sun obscured by cloud cover. Apollo, a 32-year-old male, is engrossed in grooming 26-year-old Dilly, who is holding Duke, her baby boy, and looking up. Orphan Mambo is sitting to the right of Dilly.

Dilly, 26, daughter of Beethoven. She bears a remarkable likeness to her father and is a low-ranking female who comes and goes. She disappears for a short time and then suddenly reappears with her two kids, Diaz and Duke, in tow.

One-year-old Duke at his cutest. A son of Dilly, Duke didn't at first have many opportunities to mix with other youngsters and was overwhelmed on the few occasions when the other kids tried to interact with him. A year later, he was much more confident about mixing and playing.

Diaz. Travelling with her mother Dilly, Faustino, Sandi and Sandi's children, seven-year-old Diaz pauses on the track. She has adopted a secretive lifestyle – preferring, for instance, to stay in the cover of trees when Dilly is resting on open ground.

Chapter 10: **The Ones We Lost**

During our absence from Kasekela during parts of 2012, news of several events filtered through to us.

It was finally confirmed that around April 2012 – one cannot be too sure of the date – Flirt left Kasekela Community for good and settled in the adjoining Mitumba Community to the north. Flirt's elder sister Flossi has lived in Mitumba ever since leaving Kasekela in 1996 and is now the dominant matriarch. She has four offspring – Forest, Flower, Fansi and Faldi. It was Flossi who had led the attack on Schweini when she had tried to emigrate and had sent her packing back, badly injured, to Kasekela. Flossi's treatment of other females who have tried to emigrate from Kasekela has been similarly hostile.

Nevertheless, one day in April, Flirt simply walked into Mitumba without any preliminaries. She wasn't swelling either. No one knows what exactly happened and how they knew that they were sisters but, right from the start, Flossi was friendly towards Flirt and helped her younger sister settle in Mitumba. This she accomplished by fending off any hostility from other Mitumbans. The two got on well together and Flossi even allowed Flirt to care for her kids. Fifi would have been pleased.

In January 2013, there was a border confrontation between Kasekela and Mitumba males. It was a stand-off and then, as the respective parties dispersed, Flirt appeared, apparently oblivious to the tense encounter. The hyped-up Mitumba females, who had been spectators, egged on their males to thrash Flirt. Already pumped up with heightened excitement, the males set upon Flirt and beat her up badly. She managed to get away and disappeared for a long time. She had been pregnant, but when she eventually reappeared it was minus the pregnancy. She was also skinny and had a bitten-off ear and a torn swelling. The Mitumbans acted with indifference toward her as she wisely kept either near the leader or stayed on the fringes. Flirt still has

some way to go before being fully integrated in the Mitumba Community. But Flirt is a fighter.

Then there's Mambo. Gimble had courted a Kasekelian female called Malaika and baby girl Mambo was the result. Life got off to a fine start for Mambo. But then Gimble went into a rapid decline. One day he appeared with a severe head wound and was never seen again. That was in 2007. Gimble was 30 and Mambo was two or three.

One morning in August 2009, when Mambo was five, a party of mainly male Kasekelians came across a body lying flat on the ground. Sitting next to it was little Mambo, sobbing uncontrollably. The Kasekelians were puzzled. They examined the still body, touched it, smelt it, pushed it gently, prodded it, shook it and even dragged it. It's possible they thought that Malaika, Mambo's mother, was asleep and were trying to wake her up. But Malaika was dead and the cause was surprising.

Tissue samples were taken from her body and sent to a lab. An analysis showed that the test for SIV virus had turned out to be positive. It's not clear where the virus had come from but it turned out that Gimble, too, was SIV positive. Given that both the parents were SIV positive, what lay in store for Mambo?

Mambo, orphaned at five, found life to be tough. She was neither adopted nor able to find someone she could attach herself to long-term, apart from Pax, and she would stay with the impotent male for as long as she could keep up with him. And Pax didn't appear to mind at all. Whenever she lost him, Mambo would try to attach herself to a travelling group where she was tolerated but no more – she had to find food for herself. She would earn her keep in the group by grooming everyone, but she didn't receive grooming in return. That is, except from Familia. Roughly the same age, the two girls struck up a little friendship. Familia was the only one who fussed over her and, when she did, Mambo's face lit up. Otherwise, life was lonely for

Mambo. Having lost her mother, her very identity had probably changed. She also had a tennis-ball-size growth on her right upper chest, under her arm. Was it a bacterial growth or a symptom of SIV? Perhaps SIV is taking a hold among the Kasekelians. After all, there was also the case of Yoranda, a mature female who wasted away and died. She had a fatal strain of SIV.

Alas, seven-year-old orphan Mambo was never to be seen again, reason unknown. Despite the tough life she had led after her parents had passed away, I had thought that the worst was behind her. She had only been tolerated socially but had made friends with Fanni's eldest daughter, eight-year-old Familia. In fact, Familia was never seen again either. She had begun to travel on her own for a few days at a time, unaccompanied by her mother when she disappeared without a trace. The disappearance of Mambo and Familia without any clues is a mystery. Whenever we came across Fanni during our next visit, travelling with four-year-old Fadhila and two-year-old Fifty, we noticed a subtle change. It was as if the loss of Familia had left Fanni and Fadhila more guarded.

In fact, we spent a lot of time during 2012 watching a changed Fadhila. For a four-year-old she was still very small. Nonetheless, she managed to keep up with Fanni while Fanni travelled long distances. She had also lost some hair, although otherwise she seemed fine physically. Fadhila was also more circumspect than before. The loss of her elder sister must have affected her. Fifty, on the other hand, seemed oblivious to the low-key mood of the others. Full of growing-up energy and loving the attention he was getting from from Fanni and Fadhila, he was, quite simply, a livewire.

Then we went away and, from afar, heard that the Z dynasty had suffered a loss. The Z dynasty, remember, was headed by Zrezia, along with her two sons, low-ranking Zeus and adventurous Zinda, and one shy daughter, Zella. They seemed to have been off to a good start but, in late August 2012, Zella had not been seen for several days. When she was finally found, towards the end of August, she was sleeping a lot, obviously very ill. She could hardly walk, and when she did she was unsteady on her feet. The next day she was seen with a large group of Kasekelians, curled up on the ground. The group moved on but Zella remained, asleep. She died soon after. The post-mortem showed that one of her lungs had rotted and her liver didn't look right.

Zinda, Zeus's younger brother, appeared to be all right at first but then he started sleeping a lot. He stayed in contact with his mother, Zrezia, and did manage to cover large distances with her when the group was on the move. Indeed, the Kasekelians were forming into one large group and travelling far and wide, often beyond the southern boundary of their range. Zrezia was sexually receptive and took the opportunity to flirt with all the males, young and old. We once saw her solicit mating from 12-year-old Tarzan several times by jumping up and down in front of him. Tarzan obliged. Four-year-old Google, too, was invited, and he also 'mated' with her.

As for Zinda, his face had acquired a pallor and he was resting at every opportunity. There seemed to be something not quite right with the plucky little kid who in the past had travelled on his own with the big males. A few days before we left, we couldn't find him. All we saw was Zrezia and Zeus on their own. Back in the UK we heard that Zinda couldn't be found and was presumed dead. The Z dynasty was in a sorry state: Zrezia had lost three out of her four children, with only Zeus surviving. With Zinda's death, Gimble's legacy came to an abrupt end.

We also heard that Kipara had unexpectedly passed away. I have not mentioned Kipara before for the simple reason that she was elusive. Now and then we got glimpses of her with her daughter as she went about her business in the forest, ranging on the periphery of the Community. She was born in July 1986 and was an immigrant female who briefly visited the Kasekela Community in 1997, liked what she saw, immigrated permanently in 1999 and immediately mated with all the Kasekelian males. A female baby, Kigoma, was born in July 2000 but died four months later. A second baby boy, Kobe, disappeared in 2004, aged only ten weeks, and Kipara herself was seen wounded. Matters improved when Keaton, a female baby, was born in 2005, and she and Kipara roamed together for about eight years. Then, one day in February 2013, Kipara was found, clearly dying. After her death, Keaton started tagging along with the males, especially Freud, Frodo, Ferdinand and even Titan. She is still around, managing as best as she can, hanging on in there with a little help from Pax, who had also held orphan Mambo's hand.

We saw Tubbe, a mature male, on our very first day in 2011 and then we never saw him again. We thought that perhaps he had transferred to the Kalande Community in the south, where there was said to be about ten females but only one male. But the Kalande Community is very difficult to sight and individuals are hard to identify. There have also been a steady trickle of females leaving the Community. All is not what it appears with that Community and Tubbe himself may very well be no more. If so, it's puzzling. After all, Tubbe, as I knew him, was quite capable of looking after himself. He has left at least one heir behind, though – Gimli.

Apollo, looking weak, was last seen in August 2013. Both Fiona and I have a soft spot for this lovable Kasekelian, who was small in size but big on diplomacy. He lived by his wits and got along with all the high-ranking males. The only blot on his character was when he beat up Imani, who had blundered into a frenzied Apollo after Nasa and Ferdinand had killed a baboon and Apollo had failed to get a piece of the meat. Imani was unhurt, though.

Wilkie, along with another segment of history, seems to have gone as well. Towards the end of 2012, Sandi and Wilkie disappeared for two months. Sandi reappeared but Wilkie didn't. The last time we saw him, although 39 years old then, he had looked in good condition. There was no reason to think that he would die then, but no one knows what did happen to him. Meanwhile, his heirs, Faustino, Fadhila, Gaia, Schweini and Keaton – there are others – live on. In fact, Wilkie is the most successful Kasekelian father of them all.

In May 2012, Frodo was in a sorry state. He walked slowly and avoided company. He looked thin and wasted. He had parasitic worms in his intestine that he couldn't get rid of. Instinct led him to seek every source of minerals he could find to flush away the worms, and gradually his condition improved, albeit very slowly. He began to tolerate a little company now and then, but when we had left the Kasekelians in early June, Frodo was still very weak. During our three-month absence he made a slow but sure recovery and, when we returned, we found him to be fully fit. We also found that the Kasekelians were regularly encroaching – quite boldly too – into the heart of the Kalande Community. At times with 11 big males in the lead – Ferdinand, Faustino, Frodo, Freud, Titan, Sheldon, Apollo, Wilkie, Sampson, Zeus and Fudge – they were a formidable force and met no opposition. The only young male of Kalande was nowhere to be seen, and the females had begun transferring to Kasekela. Kati, Makiwa and Mgeni were the latest additions so that, despite the loss of Mambo, Familia, Tubbe and Wilkie, the Kasekela population remained stable. Of course, its land size was bigger, since the annexation of Kalande territory was now a formality.

Frodo had, indeed, made a full recovery and was travelling huge distances with the others. He was also getting involved in social situations. One day we were with the nine G's – they were draped around a termite mound, termite-fishing, resting, and playing – when Frodo walked in. Gaia and the kids rushed to greet him and Glitter went to groom him. Gimli groomed him too and Google rushed up to him and got an intense hug. But Gremlin and Golden continued with their activities. After all the greeting and grooming was over, Frodo sat alone, as if pondering his next move. After a while, he got up and displayed at Gremlin and Golden, perhaps reminding them not to ignore him, and they apologised to him at once. He sat down again and Glitter proceeded to calm him down further by grooming him. This incident was, in some ways, reminiscent of the younger Frodo, when he was the leader and did as he pleased, spreading terror among the Kasekelians.

In late 2012, as we watched a reinvigorated Frodo, I thought his metamorphosis had been most profound. He was clearly an elder statesman, respected by the males, loved by the kids, sought after by the females – not the Frodo who was once a bully and shunned and who had nearly died 11 years earlier. This, I thought, was resurrection.

But, exactly a year later, he was again thin and emaciated. He walked slowly and covered only a little ground, unable to keep up with a travelling group. It seemed that his previous ailment had re-emerged. Somehow he survived and, in fact, perked up for a while; his eyes shone and he looked more like the Frodo we used to know, though he was still thin. One day he tried to rejoin the group but when Ferdinand saw his elder brother, he felt obliged to remind Frodo who was the boss. He set upon Frodo and was joined by Faustino. Frodo cried and begged for mercy. When Ferdinand left him alone, unhurt, a few Kasekelians gathered around him, consoling a whimpering Frodo and grooming him with affection.

That was the last time we saw Frodo in good condition. When we returned to the modern world, on 10 November, we received the news that Frodo had died that day. Fiona broke down with an outpouring of grief. She had a soft spot for him but it was also because he was life. I remembered him as the unassailable leader and then as a mature elder statesman, still full of the symphony of the living. An era had ended.

Apollo eating mango. It's October and the mango season is well under way. The Kasekelians, travelling as a group, had made straight for a mango tree near the shore of Lake Tanganyika. The males fed first and then promptly fell asleep.

Flirt calling. When Fifi died, leaving six-year-old Flirt behind, it was
Frodo and an old female called Candy who leant her a helping hand.
She got through to puberty and then adjusted to being on her own
for long spells at a time, staying near the border between Kasekela
Community and Mitumba Community. Then, one day in April 2012,
Flirt left her natal home and settled in Mitumba Community where
her elder sister, Flossi, is the dominant matriarch.

Frodo calling. After he lost the leadership Frodo managed to rehabilitate himself in the Community and adapted to being a marginal player. It was surprising, given the despotic nature of his rule, that he became a popular figure among the females and the kids.

Fifty at seven months (right) and Fifty at three years (above). Precocious seven-month-old Fifty, Fanni's baby boy, was used to being fussed over. Fanni, in particular, doted on him. Fifty was 18 months old when older sister Familia disappeared. While this left Fanni and Fadhila markedly subdued, irrepressible Fifty was oblivious to the loss. He grew fast and, as he has grown, he has become more daring and adventurous.

Mambo. Seven-year-old Mambo was an orphan. She lost her father, Gimble, when she was two and half years old, and her mother, Malaika, when she was five. Mambo then attached herself to whoever would tolerate her, in particular the old standby, Pax. Fortunately, Mambo had been weaned and Pax was excellent at finding food.

Kipara. She was elusive. She ranged on the periphery of the Community, making it difficult to know her and her daughter, Keaton. She died unexpectedly in February 2013, cause unknown.

Pax at 36 with 8-year-old Keaton. After Keaton
lost her mother, Kipara, the males took it in turns
to lend her a helping hand, but it was Pax who
looked after her the most.

Keaton. For a juvenile orphan, Keaton appears to
be quite confident. She has no trouble finding food
or keeping up with a fast-travelling group.

Apollo and Wilkie. Both Apollo, on the right, and Wilkie retired from the hierarchical rat race a long time ago, content to lead lives indifferent to social status. Their interest in sex, however, remained. Both were healthy and highly capable of looking after themselves, so their disappearance, first Wilkie and then Apollo, is a puzzle.

Frodo resting. In May 2012 Frodo was in a sorry state, looking thin and wasted. He walked slowly for only short distances and avoided company. When we saw Frodo again four months later, he had made a seemingly complete recovery from what turned out to be a parasitic infection of the intestines. He was regularly travelling long distances with a large group led by the males and taking part in social affairs. He also sneaked in a few copulations.

Frodo hugging Google. All the young ones appeared to have an emotional attachment to Frodo. In turn, he found time for them. Here he is hugging Google, who ran to him on a sudden impulse. We have seen many such instances, including little Ipo running to him and being kissed by Frodo on the cheek, and Frodo playing a game with Gizmo that involved going round and round in circles – with great animation too.

Frodo. These pictures were taken less than a month before Frodo died. He had been ill again but was showing signs of recovery. Although far from fully fit, he decided to join the group of Kasekelians we were with. Upon spotting Frodo, Ferdinand attacked him, as did Faustino. Frodo sobbed uncontrollably but was unhurt physically. A few Kasekelians, including Fudge and Tabora in the picture, gathered around him and tried to console him. Frodo cheered up after a while but didn't rejoin the group. We thought he was okay but he died on 10 November 2013.

Chapter 11: **The Male Hierarchy**

One day, in the month of October 2012, we sat with the males. In the centre, grooming with serious intent, were the four F boys. Titan joined in but soon went to one side and lay down. None of the adolescents like Tarzan or Fundi dared to go near the four F's. The young ones sat about 10 yards away, transfixed with reverence.

It's evident that the grip of the F's on the leadership is tight. Ferdinand is still the leader, with his elder brother Faustino at number two. Even now, I cannot believe how easily and naturally the skinny Ferdinand I knew as a kid has transformed into a powerful yet mature and intelligent leader. Sometimes I feel he knows it.

When it comes to being in charge, Ferdinand is a maestro. Whenever there is any dispute among the females, he only has to show himself for the dispute to subside. In fact, whenever Ferdinand walks into a social group, everyone, including all the males, greets him submissively. And Ferdinand, in his mysterious way, makes sure it stays that way. Consider the following incident.

One cloudy morning we were walking along the beach with the Kasekelians when we came across a troop of colobus monkeys atop a tree. The Kasekelians stopped and waited, taking their time, looking for an opportunity to strike. But then it started to rain and the colobus hunt was abandoned. Ferdinand calmly got up and worked himself up to perform a stunning rain dance. He pranced around, fully fluffed up, throwing leaves, sticks and stones. He broke branches, charged in straight lines and moved in circles. It was unlike a normal, charging display, and it went on for a long time, 15 or so minutes. All the Kasekelians, some from the safety of trees, watched, stupefied. Having made his point about who was the boss, Ferdinand sat down, thoroughly pleased with himself.

Turning to Faustino, he had been thought of as leadership material in the past but today appears to be content with being at number two. Although, whenever Ferdinand leaves the centre of the Community, Faustino takes charge and keeps order by frequent displays. In fact, at times Faustino seems to be out of control as he displays all over the place in his enthralling style. Clearly, for the moment, the two brothers are working harmoniously to keep the leadership firmly entrenched in the F dynasty. Together, they are unbeatable. However, it's worth noting that Faustino is friendly with Titan when Ferdinand is not around. But as soon as Ferdinand appears, Faustino turns his back on Titan.

When Ferdinand and Faustino are absent, Titan is the Kasekelian to be most wary of. He is capable of creating havoc, sending Kasekelians screaming up trees with his frightening displays and uncertain temper. But when Ferdinand is there, Titan is so meek that once he let himself be intimidated by nine-year-old Gimli rather than risk the displeasure of Ferdinand, who had a soft spot for Gimli. In fact, it looks as if Ferdinand may 'sponsor' Gimli, looking after him when in the company of the males and ensuring Gimli doesn't get into trouble with them. Although Titan is big and strong – in fact, the biggest and strongest of them all – he is a mental wreck in Ferdinand's presence. But when it comes to claiming leadership, there are a lot of factors at play, such as Ferdinand being laid low by an unexpected illness, thereby providing Titan with an opportunity to overthrow him, or Faustino staying neutral in a Ferdinand-Titan fight. So I suppose it's better to wait and see than predict and get it wrong. The thing about the Kasekelians is that their history, really a history of diverse personalities cooperating and colliding, is no guide to what will happen. It's best to be wise after the event. One thing is clear, however. Titan, if he wants to mount a serious challenge, could do with controlling his wayward impulses and improving his diplomatic skills. Quite simply, he is not building alliances, winning friends and influencing Kasekelians. The potential of having a formidable ally in his full brother, Tarzan, is there, but he isn't exploiting it.

So Titan is still at number three, while number four is occupied by Sheldon. The big surprise is that 16-year-old Fudge has climbed to number five in the rankings.

Fudge's climb was facilitated by the fact that a few males were out of the running, either by choice or by circumstance. Wilkie and Apollo had lost interest in hierarchical matters long ago (and, as previously mentioned, have both since disappeared). The same lack of interest applied to Freud. To him, it seems, it was a matter of leaving it to the younger generation.

Towards the end of our visit in October 2011, we met up with Freud who was in a sorry state. You could tell at once that he was very lethargic. We watched him build a nest in a fruiting tree and sleep. Occasionally he would drag himself to nibble a fruit and, whenever he walked on ground, it was painfully slow. As time passed his misery grew worse. He could hardly manage a couple of steps, and so he would just lie on the ground, sleeping. It was sad to watch my favourite Kasekelian like this, but perhaps Freud would bounce back and we would find him well and fully functioning when we returned.

Freud did indeed make a dramatic recovery after he had been slipped a course of antibiotics. He became fully fit again and promptly reverted to his lonesome ways, occasionally travelling with the males, quietly slinking in and slinking away, always on his own terms. Then he sprang a surprise. He persuaded Tanga to go on a consortship with him, and the two, with little Tabora in tow, left for an extended sojourn at the edge of the Community's range.

Freud's return to good health did not last. In April 2014 we were in the United Kingdom checking the first proofs of this book when we heard that Freud had unexpectedly died at one of his favourite spots above Kakombe valley, apparently peacefully and in a gentlemanly style. If Freud ever thought about dying then perhaps this is the manner he would have chosen.

And so to Ferdinand, who clearly relishes being the leader. During the last phase of our last trip there were five females ready and willing to mate, and Ferdinand had the pick of them. However, Ferdinand was being choosy – his mind was on Sandi. He and Sandi were always together and, whenever the other females presented themselves to Ferdinand, he simply ignored them. Things, though, are not always what they seem and perhaps Ferdinand loves something more than Sandi – for consider the incident that we witnessed while travelling with a group of about 40 Kasekelians.

During their travels, the group normally took in several mango trees that were bearing fruit. When the big group Ferdinand and Sandi were in came to the mango tree at Nyasanga, every Kasekelian gathered up fallen mangoes and sat down to eat them. After a while, Sandi came to Ferdinand and invited him to copulate. Ferdinand thought for a minute, picked up his stash of mangoes, went to Sandi, put the mangoes down, mated with Sandi, picked up the mangoes and went away to eat in peace. Having finished eating his mangoes, Ferdinand went to his elder sister Fanni who was sitting with a stash of mangoes, happily eating. Ferdinand felt each of Fanni's mangoes, took the one he fancied and walked off with it. One of the benefits of being the leader is presumably also having the pick of the mangoes.

Faustino is the one who normally shows the greatest excitement whenever the Kasekelians come across food. On another occasion, a storm the previous day had shaken a mango tree, resulting in many fallen mangoes. When the group came to them, with the males in the lead, they went mad. The males charged, vocalised and hugged each other. Faustino was the most excited, squealing loudly and continuously and charging at any juvenile or female that dared to come near the fruit.

Faustino ate a lot of mangoes that day. As he sat next to Fanni, with a bloated tummy and a stash in front of him, Fanni gingerly reached out and took a mango from the stash. Faustino, full up, let her. He couldn't be bothered.

We also saw Fanni during the last days of our trip, often with Fifty on her back and Fadhila following, as she went about foraging. Occasionally, her sons Fundi and Fudge would turn up and spend some time with her. She seemed comfortable in the niche she had created for herself. Her contribution to Fifi's legacy is already significant. Moreover, given her reproductive prowess, she is likely to deliver more little F's in the future. Her younger sister in the Mitumba Community – Flossi – is like her in that she is already a mother of four F's and is likely to match Fanni's production in the future.

I sat on the beach, surrounded by our bags and gear. The lake was calm and the forest behind silent. As we waited for the boat to arrive, the atmosphere got me thinking. We had spent a lot of time with the Kasekelians and got to know them individually. We had discovered depth to their personalities which is perhaps why they get to us. Yet there was something else, some openness, naivety, straightforwardness, innocence that lay behind their attraction. With them, you got what you saw.

The boat came to pick us up. It was time to leave this strange world inhabited by a strange tribe with its own peculiar way of living but somehow living life to the full at a leisurely pace. We reluctantly headed back to our own little existence, mired in concrete, technology, speed, superficiality and mumbo jumbo – but an existence that, for us, had been inexplicably enriched by the world we were leaving behind.

Ferdinand feeding in a tree. There was a movement and, looking up, we saw Ferdinand high up in a large forest tree, calmly munching some leaves. Nearby we could hear the murmur of a little stream flowing down to the lake. It was a fine evening with which to finish a day in the forest in the company of the Kasekelians.

Faustino (on the left), Ferdinand (in the middle) and Apollo.
They had been resting and grooming when a faint call
propelled them to move to its source. After a few days of
our arrival in Kasekela that September 2012, we had worked
out that Ferdinand was very much in command, with elder
brother Faustino firmly entrenched at number two. Apollo
was just a low-ranking male, tolerated by the brothers.

Faustino calling. Whenever Ferdinand left the centre of the Community, elder brother Faustino stayed behind and took charge, keeping order with frequent displays. Here, he got up from a grooming session, started vocalising and then got everyone else to stop whatever they were engaged in and to follow his lead and move on.

Faustino leading the boys. Ferdinand was away on an amorous mission which meant that Faustino was once again in charge. Here, he leads Titan, Frodo and Tarzan with unquestioned authority.

Titan calling (left). Titan, who had been resting with the other males, joins in the chorus of calling in response to calls initiated by Faustino. Titan has contrasting sides to his personality: he can be a team player but he usually chooses to wander alone; he bullies many but grovels before Ferdinand; he interacts well with Faustino but treats his sister Tanga with disdain.

Titan hugging Ferdinand (right). Whenever Titan came across Ferdinand, he was quite subservient. Here, he rushed to greet and hug Ferdinand from behind – a most peculiar Titan eccentricity – to seek the reassurance of a friendly response from Ferdinand. Ferdinand, astute as ever, deliberately ignored Titan, thereby strengthening his psychological hold over his rival.

Previous pages: Fudge grooming Apollo. The place is a clearing high up called Hilltop, where a cluster of trees had started bearing fruit. Fifteen-year-old Fudge, already ranked above 32-year-old Apollo at number five, has been able to climb quickly up the male hierarchy partly because a few males, including Apollo, had opted for a quieter life.

Freud (above). When he was in his prime, Freud mated more than any other Kasekelian. Puzzlingly, he has not sired any of the living Kasekelian youngsters. DNA analysis shows that he did sire one baby, at least, which died. So it seems that he is not impotent, but he doesn't appear to have any heirs.

Frodo. Frodo mated less than Freud when in his prime yet, among the known Kasekela males, has sired the second highest number of babies. Frodo had a huge appetite for sex when he was the leader. Once, he wanted to take a reluctant Gremlin on a consortship. Gremlin dithered; Frodo lost his cool and beat her up savagely. Gremlin had no choice but to comply with his wishes.

Fudge and Freud. Although 16-year-old nephew Fudge (sitting up) is ranked higher than his 42-year-old uncle Freud, he shows touching respect for the wise, great Kasekelian whenever they chance to meet. But then Fudge is like that – a nice male popular with everyone. Here, he had been grooming Freud before the interruption of a call, heard and responded to.

Mango feast. From left to right : dozing Faustino with a pile of uneaten mangoes; Fanni methodically going through her heap of mangoes; Fifty, who has yet to develop a taste for the fruit, swinging on the tree above; Fadhila; and Siri. As soon as the moving group of Kasekelians had come near the mango tree, the males in the lead yelled and screamed and charged around with elation at the prospect of a feast. Each one quickly picked up the fallen mangoes and ate to satiation.

311

Frodo taking the lead. It's mid-morning and the males are sleeping after feeding and socialising. A fully fit Frodo is the first to make a move, picking his way through the prone bodies. Soon after Frodo's departure, the others stirred and headed in the direction Frodo had taken, up a slope and beyond to fruiting trees.

Faustino leads. It's a cloudy afternoon and Faustino is leading a small group of Kasekelians. They had been to the southern part of their home and are on their way back to the centre.

Ferdinand and elder brother Faustino. The brothers
are number one and two in the male hierarchy.
They were travelling together and paused to take in
the panorama before them. Finding no one within
their sight, they continued their long walk towards
the Mitumba Community border.

Dynasty Trees

The **S** Dynasty

Sparrow ♀ (1958)

- Sandi ♀ (10.1973)
- Sheldon ♂ (05.1983)
- Schweini ♀ (04.1991)
  (Father: Wilkie)
- Spud ♂ (05.1996) ⊗
- Sinbad ♂ (06.2001)
  (Father: Frodo)

Sandi ♀ (10.1973):
- Sherehe ♀
  (01.1991–05.11.2006) ⊗
  - Infant ⊗
- Sampson ♂ (04.1996)
  (Father: Apollo)
- Samwise ♀ (06.2001)
  (Father: Frodo)
- Siri ♂ (02.2007)
  (Father: Apollo)

Schweini ♀ (04.1991):
- Baby S (09.2007) ⊗
- Safi ♀
  (16.10.2008–08.2011) ⊗
- Shwali ♂ (11.2012)

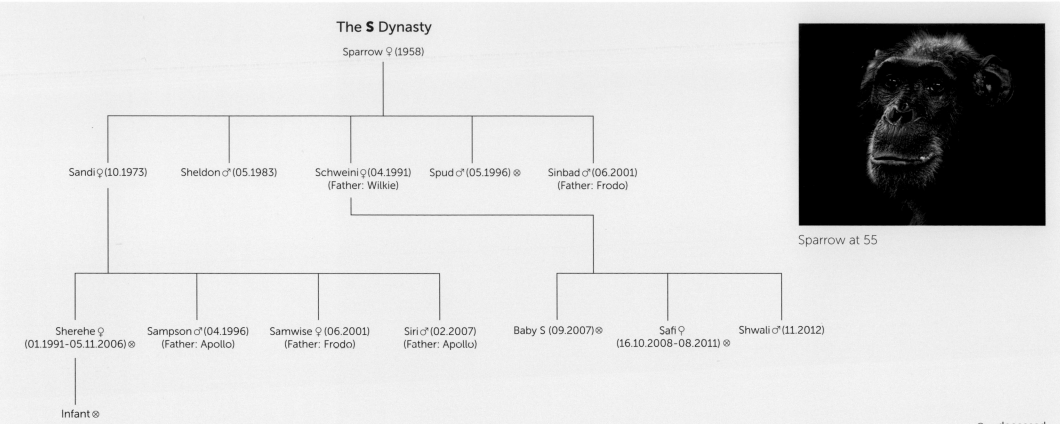

Sparrow at 55

⊗ = deceased

The **T** Dynasty

Tatti ♀ (06.1961) ⊗
(Also known as Patti)

- Tita ♀ (01.1984) ⊗
- Tanga ♀ (04.1989)
  (Father: Goblin)
- Titan ♂ (08.1994)
  (Father: Frodo)
- Tarzan ♂ (10.1999)
  (Father: Frodo)

Tanga ♀ (04.1989):
- Tom ♂ (03.2001)
  (Father: Kris)
- Tabora ♀ (2007)
  (Father: Ferdinand)
- Tarime ♀ (07.10.2012–08.2013) ⊗

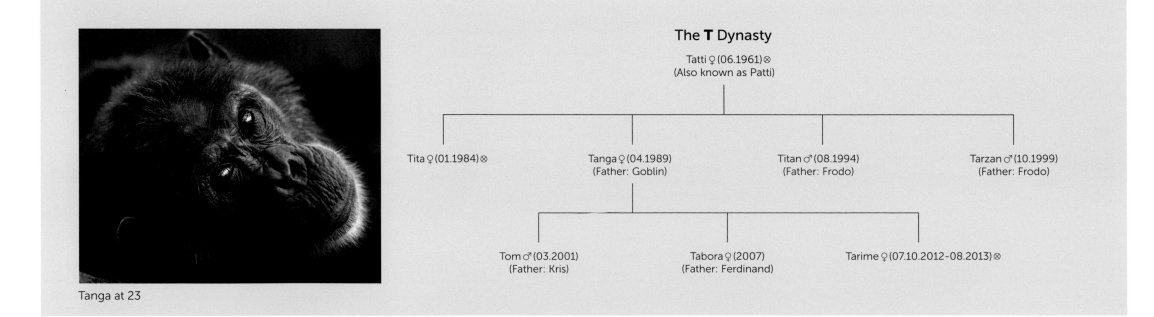

Tanga at 23

The **F** Dynasty

Fifi ♀ (06.1958-08.2004) ⊗

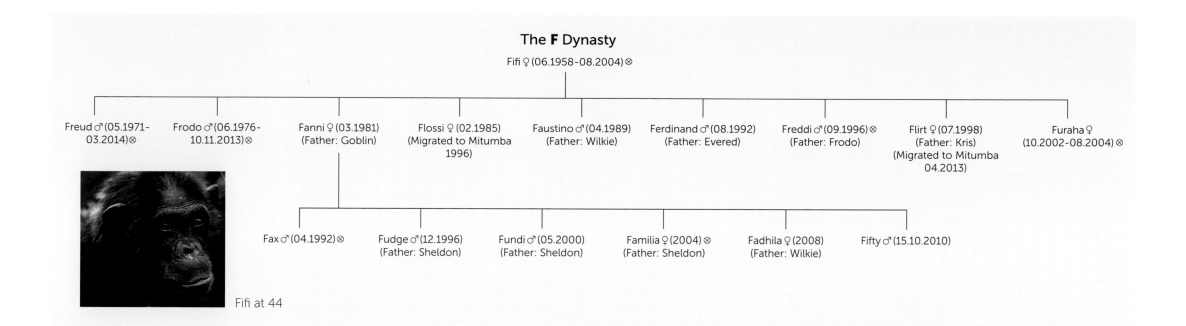

| Freud ♂ (05.1971-03.2014) ⊗ | Frodo ♂ (06.1976-10.11.2013) ⊗ | Fanni ♀ (03.1981) (Father: Goblin) | Flossi ♀ (02.1985) (Migrated to Mitumba 1996) | Faustino ♂ (04.1989) (Father: Wilkie) | Ferdinand ♂ (08.1992) (Father: Evered) | Freddi ♂ (09.1996) ⊗ (Father: Frodo) | Flirt ♀ (07.1998) (Father: Kris) (Migrated to Mitumba 04.2013) | Furaha ♀ (10.2002-08.2004) ⊗ |

Fanni ♀ children:

| Fax ♂ (04.1992) ⊗ | Fudge ♂ (12.1996) (Father: Sheldon) | Fundi ♂ (05.2000) (Father: Sheldon) | Familia ♀ (2004) ⊗ (Father: Sheldon) | Fadhila ♀ (2008) (Father: Wilkie) | Fifty ♂ (15.10.2010) |

Fifi at 44

The **G** Dynasty

Gremlin ♀ (11.1970) (Father: Evered)

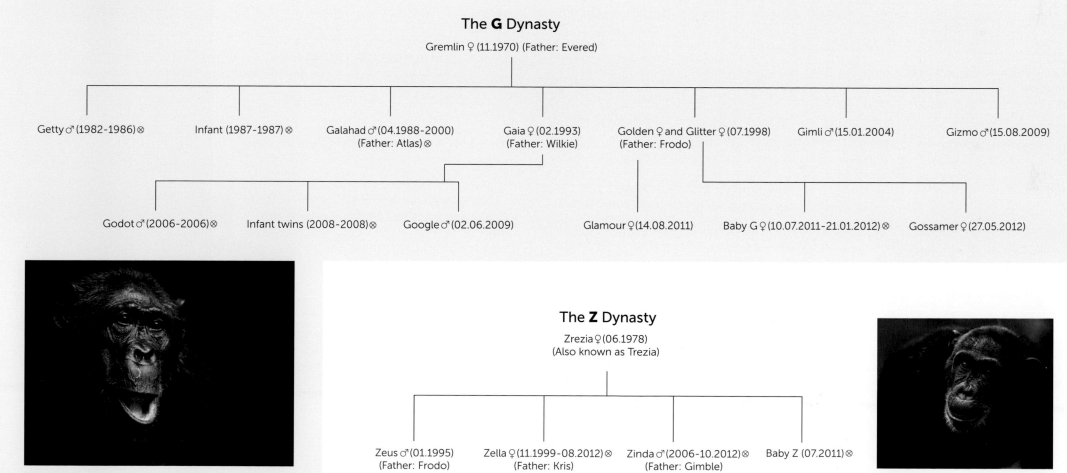

| Getty ♂ (1982-1986) ⊗ | Infant (1987-1987) ⊗ | Galahad ♂ (04.1988-2000) (Father: Atlas) ⊗ | Gaia ♀ (02.1993) (Father: Wilkie) | Golden ♀ and Glitter ♀ (07.1998) (Father: Frodo) | Gimli ♂ (15.01.2004) | Gizmo ♂ (15.08.2009) |

| Godot ♂ (2006-2006) ⊗ | Infant twins (2008-2008) ⊗ | Google ♂ (02.06.2009) | Glamour ♀ (14.08.2011) | Baby G ♀ (10.07.2011-21.01.2012) ⊗ | Gossamer ♀ (27.05.2012) |

Gremlin at 41

The **Z** Dynasty

Zrezia ♀ (06.1978)
(Also known as Trezia)

| Zeus ♂ (01.1995) (Father: Frodo) | Zella ♀ (11.1999-08.2012) ⊗ (Father: Kris) | Zinda ♂ (2006-10.2012) ⊗ (Father: Gimble) | Baby Z (07.2011) ⊗ |

Zrezia at 34

319

Leaders at Kasekela

1961–1964 Goliath
Goliath was a large male with an uncertain temper. He also had a fast-charging display and it helped in holding on to his leadership that he had a reliable ally in David Greybeard. He was a popular leader.

1964–early 1971 Mike
Mike was actually relatively small and not expected to be a leader. But he was shrewd. He used tin cans that he found lying around in camp, which were foreign to the Kasekelian Society, to produce a terrifying noise while displaying – he could roll three five-gallon kerosene cans in front of him as he charged through a group. The loud clanging terrified the Kasekelians. When the tin cans were removed, Mike incorporated chairs, tables, boxes and tripods in his displays, and the change to the social order was irreversible. Mike became the leader without a fight. What might the subsequent history of the Kasekelians have been had the tin cans not been there? What profound changes in social dynamics would have occurred further down the line?

Early 1971-November 1972 (20 months) Humphrey
Humphrey was big, strong and powerful. More brawn than brain, he was a loyal ally of Mike when Figan, elder brother of Fifi, and Evered were showing clear insubordination to Mike. But ambition is made of sterner stuff, and Humphrey was finally mentally strong enough to take Mike on when he had become thinner and his teeth had been ground down and canines broken. One morning Mike was quietly feeding by himself when Humphrey, backed by temporary ally Faben, elder brother of Figan, charged at him and pounded him brutally. Mike took refuge in a tree, but Humphrey pursued him there, dragged him down and beat him up, with Faben joining in. From then on, Humphrey was the leader.

November 1972-May 1973 — No clear leader.
Humphrey, Evered and Figan competed for leadership.

May 1973 – mid-1979 Figan
The elder brother of Fifi, Figan had a clear goal right from an early age: he wanted the leadership. He planned and schemed, and then, having nurtured an alliance with his elder brother, Faben, he took on Evered and Humphrey separately on several occasions.

Loyally backed by Faben, his strategy paid off and he became the undisputed leader, reigning for just over six years.

Mid 1979-1984 – No clear leader.
Goblin was a determined and ambitious lad who started the process of dominating the females from about the age of 10. By 13, he had challenged and finally dominated the toughest female, Gigi. He then turned to the males and began testing them. Goblin had a sponsor in the then alpha male, Figan, who looked out for him when he got into too much trouble. While rising in rank, Goblin would hide in thickets and burst out in a terrifying charge when the others approached. He would also rise before dawn and display over his sleepy rivals. In other words, Goblin played dirty.

Finally, the climb upwards came to a point at which Figan and Goblin, tutor and pupil, competed for leadership during the period mid-1979 to July 1982. Figan disappeared in July 1982, and you could argue that until his disappearance he was the leader. Although Goblin was always on top in one-on-one confrontations, he could be challenged successfully by Figan and another male acting together. After Figan's disappearance, Goblin was once again on top when it came to one-on-one confrontations but couldn't defeat the coalitions that continued to oppose him.

1984-October 25, 1989 Goblin
Goblin finally became the undisputed leader, having simply tired out all his opponents. He ruled with a ruthless streak, used terror tactics and brooked no opposition.

October 28, 1989-February 8, 1993 Wilkie
Wilkie, with the support of his mother, quickly rose to be a high-ranking male. He wasn't particularly big or strong, but he was astute and hungry for power. In a remarkable battle with Goblin, he came out on top and became the leader. Goblin was very badly injured in the fight. When he had recovered, Goblin tried again but was set upon by Wilkie and a few other males acting together, again hurting him almost fatally.

February 8, 1993-September 29, 1997 Freud
With the backing of his mother, Fifi, Freud climbed rapidly to number two position. There he languished for some time before making an unexpected challenge to Wilkie. Freud

won, became the leader and then ruled with a light touch. The only viable challenger was his younger brother, Frodo.

October 2, 1997-early January 2003 Frodo
Frodo, the second heaviest Kasekelian in living memory, rose to the second highest position through sheer strength. Yet, when it came to dislodging his elder brother Freud from the top position, he lacked the mental edge. Then Freud fell ill and Frodo walked in as the leader. Frodo ruled like a bully initially but then settled into a more benign role. He looked set to be the leader for a long time, simply because there were no suitable challengers. Then, in December 2002, Frodo, along with several other males, became ill and emaciated. He turned into a recluse while slowly recovering.

Early January 2003-late 2003 — No clear leader.
Frodo left a vacuum into which Sheldon, Kris, Apollo, Gimble and Freud tried to step. This was a period of flux in which alliances were tested and discarded. Then Apollo fell ill, Kris became weak with an infection, Freud lost interest and, as Sheldon dominated Gimble, he became leader by default.

Dec 7, 2002 – 15 Nov 2004 (estimated) Sheldon
Sheldon was a weak leader and by the middle of 2004 had had enough of the role. He left the centre of the group to spend time away.

16 Nov 2004 – 15 Mar 2008 (estimated) Kris
Kris stepped in as a leader. Slowly he consolidated his grip and then ruled in a gracious manner until he was challenged by the highly intelligent but utterly ruthless Ferdinand.

March 2008-present Ferdinand
Having forged an alliance with his elder brother Faustino, Ferdinand launched a series of unexpected attacks on Kris and reduced him to a nervous wreck. Kris disappeared and Ferdinand became the leader. So far, no one has challenged him as he rules with a firm and calculated touch.

Right:Ferdinand, the current leader. He has, in fact, been the leader since March 2008.

Titan. Rival to Ferdinand the leader, Titan takes
it easy for the moment.

Resources

Books

Boyd, William, *Brazzaville Beach*, Penguin Books, 1990

Goodall, Jane, *In the Shadow of Man*, Boston: Houghton Miffin, 1971

Goodall, Jane, *The Chimpanzees of Gombe: Patterns of Behaviour*, Cambridge, MA: Belknap Press of the Harvard University Press, 1986

Goodall, Jane, *Through a Window: 30 years Observing The Gombe Chimpanzee*s, Boston: Houghton Miffin, 1990

Jahme, Carole, *Beauty and the beast: Woman, Ape and Evolution*, London, Virago Press, 2000

Morrell, Virginia, *Ancestral Passions: The Leakey Family and The Quest for Humankind's Beginnings*, New York: Simon & Schuster, 1995

Packer, Craig, *Into Africa*, Chicago: The University of Chicago Press, 1994

Raffaele, Paul, *Among the Great Apes: Adventures on the Trail of Our Closest Relatives*, Harper Collins, 2011

Television and Film

People of the Forest: The Chimpanzees of Gombe, Hugo van Lawick, National Geographic Society, 1988

Chimpanzee Alert, Nature Watch series, Central TV, 1990

Chimpanzees: So Like Us, HBO, 1990

Fifi's Boys: A Story of Wild Chimpanzees, Natural World Series, BBC, 1996

Chimpanzee Diary, Animal Zone, BBC, 1998-9

Year of the Chimpanzee, Bill Wallauer, Survival Anglia, 2003

Almost Human, Creative Differences, Animal Planet/ Discovery Communications, 2007